THE STEP BY STEP ART OF

Dried Flowers

Published by
CHARTWELL BOOKS, INC.
A Division of **BOOK SALES, INC.**
110 Enterprise Avenue
Secaucus, New Jersey 07094

CLB 3111
© 1993 CLB Publishing, Godalming, Surrey, England
Printed and bound in Singapore by Tien Wah Press
All rights reserved
ISBN 1-55521-886-5

Text and Floral Designs by
MING VEEVERS-CARTER

Photography by
STEVE TANNER

THE STEP BY STEP ART OF
Dried Flowers

CHARTWELL
BOOKS, INC.

Contents

Introduction

Dried flowers are no longer dull and lifeless winter substitutes for the abundance of fresh flowers available in the spring, summer and autumn. Improved techniques for drying have made commercially-dried flowers vibrant in colour, strong in shape and wide in variety. This high quality dried plant material lends itself to creating truly stunning and unique displays and decorations for the home for long-lasting pleasure, as exemplified by the designs in this book. However, many types of garden flower and foliage can be simply and successfully dried at home, which can be used in conjunction with exotic, commercially-dried items. Woods and waysides offer a rich harvest of cones and nuts, seedheads, pods and fungi for use in arrangements. Even artificial fruits and flowers can be imaginatively combined with natural dried material to produce richly-coloured displays.

Commercial Drieds

An increasingly wide range of commercially-dried plant material is available from a number of sources – florist and gift shops, department stores and garden centres. Dried flowers can also be mail-ordered together with all kinds of interesting dried items such as cones, lychin, moss, seedheads and pods, preserved leaves and fruits. Dried flowers are normally sold in bunches of one type, although occasionally mixed bunches are available, especially from gift shops. Cones, seedheads and pods can often be bought singly. Pot pourri mixtures, which are readily available, can be a good source of interesting and exotic cones and pods.

Before purchasing bunches of dried material, check the size and condition of each bunch. Select full-sized bunches that have not been flattened or squashed in any way. To test for damage, hold the bunch upside-down and shake gently (not vigorously!) to ensure that the flowers are not brittle and broken. Look for strength of colour in the flowers and check that it has not faded by comparing the colour of the outer flowers in the bunch with the ones in the centre.

Dyed Drieds

These are widely available in shops along with the natural-coloured material but I personally avoid using them since the colours tend to be overpowering and highly unnatural. Common dyed drieds include Gypsophila and a range of ornamental grasses such as quaking and pearl grass, rye and gypsy grass, as well as cereals such as oats and barley. Some of these items are also available in a bleached form.

Artificial Drieds

Poly-dried flowers have arrived relatively recently on the artificial flower market. They are made from polyester and heated to make the fabric shrivel slightly to give a dried flower appearance and texture. They have some advantages in that they are washable, highly durable and do not have to be wired as much as natural dried flowers for use in arrangements and decorations. However, they cannot quite emulate the effect of real dried flowers.

Paper and other kinds of artificial flowers can be used effectively in combination with natural dried items. Artificial fruits are also highly decorative. Do not be put off by their often crude-looking stems and leaves; judge the appearance of the fruit alone. Early in the new year is an ideal time to stock up on artificial items since many stores sell off excess Christmas stock cheaply.

Selection

The following pages present a selection of the most effective dried flowers, chosen for their shape, texture and colour, which can be purchased ready-dried or dried in the home (see pages 16-17).

Above: *Bunches of colourful* Helichrysum *being commercially air-dried.*

Rosa *'Minuet'* Celosia Rosa *'Jaguar'*

Rosa *'Mercedes'* *Dark purple* Helichrysum *Salmon* Helichrysum

Yellow Achillea   Sunflower   Button chrysanthemum

Morrison   Carthamus   Rosa *'Golden Times'*

Rosa *'Vivaldi'* Peony Rosa *'Gerdo'*

Rosa *'Pink Delight'* Protea Rosa *'Kiss'*

Lilac Larkspur   *Baby* Eucalyptus   *Lilac* Achillea

Marjoram   Ageratum   *Lavender*

Home-preserved Drieds

Air-drying

This is the easiest and cheapest method of preserving plant material, although some plants are better preserved by using desiccants or glycerine (see below). Plants should be harvested on a dry day after any dew has evaporated. They should be grouped in small bunches, the stems bound together tightly near their bases with an elastic band (string can be used for woody stems since they are unlikely to shrink) and hung upside-down in a dry, dark and well-ventilated interior. A boiler or empty airing cupboard, a warm attic or over a radiator are all ideal sites. Leave the flowers to dry for several days – the exact length of time will vary according to atmospheric conditions and the type of plant. Check thoroughly to make sure that the flowers are completely dry before use.
Lavender must be harvested just before

the buds begin to burst into flower. Dock flowers, cow parsley, roses and peonies should be cut when the blooms are at their peak. Make sure hydrangea heads are firm to the touch. These flowers, together with delphiniums, are best dried singly. Always dry more than you need since there will probably be some casualties.

Rose heads and other single flowerheads as well as tulip petals can be dried in a conventional oven on a very low heat. Keep checking the flowers to prevent them from browning.

Desiccants

These drying agents – sand, borax or silica gel – draw moisture from plants to preserve them. Silica gel, the most effective and the most expensive desiccant, is available usually in the form of white crystals from chemist shops or hardware stores. The stems of flowers to be dried in this

way must be trimmed to 2.5 cm (1 in) in length. Insert a short stub wire inside each stalk while the flowers are fresh to minimise handling once they have been dried since they can be very brittle. A longer length of wire can then be bound onto the wire if necessary (see pages 24-25). Place a layer of crystals in the bottom of an airtight container and position flowers on the crystals (they should not be touching each other). Using a spoon, carefully cover the flowers with the crystals, inside and around each bloom, taking care not to distort their shape. When fully covered, replace the lid of the container and store in a warm place for about 48 hours. Unearth the flowers with great care to avoid damage.

For quick results, put the crystals in a shallow microwave-proof dish, add flowerheads and place in a microwave oven. 'Cook' on the highest setting for 5 to 7 minutes, checking every 30 seconds when almost ready. Leave the flowers to cool in the crystals for about 10-15 minutes before removing.

Borax is a cheaper desiccant but takes longer to work – about 10 days. Mix with dry silver sand, three parts borax to two parts sand, and use in the same way as the silica gel.

Use desiccants to preserve roses, peonies, lilies, freesias, fuschias and anemones.

Glycerining

This method is best used to preserve deciduous and evergreen foliage. Make a mixture of one part glycerine to two parts boiling water and pour into a fairly tall, narrow container. Stand stems in about 8-10 cm (3-4 in) of the mixture. Hammer the ends of woody stems to facilitate absorption. Leave for a week and check leaves for pliability. Some stems may require longer treatment. Individual leaves can be glycerined by immersing entirely in the mixture in a shallow container. Some flowerheads can be effectively preserved in this way, such as roses and anemones.

Right: *A bunch of roses in their fresh state and after being air-dried. The blooms shrink a good deal but also open out a little after they have been hanging up. The colours have been well preserved although they do change in hue.*

17

Equipment

Dry florist's foam is generally essential in making an arrangement. There are blocks that can be easily cut and shaped to fit containers, as a base in which to position stems (see opposite); balls of varying sizes which can be used for topiaries (page 26), rose or bay balls (pages 58 and 23); cones which can also be used for topiaries (page 114) and rings used as a base for wreaths (pages 68-69). Nylon-reinforced plaster is ideal for setting trunks in pots when making topiaries (page 26). A glue gun is an excellent tool and can be used to glue all kinds of items onto wreaths, baskets, wood and fabric. The glue is hot so extra care must be taken to avoid burning the fingers. There are various different types and thicknesses of wire (page 25), but I only use four kinds: narrow and thick silver wire for fine work, for example headdresses (the thicker is best); 22 gauge stem wires, which are long and narrow, used for wiring light bunches or single stems; and 18 gauge stem wires, which are thicker versions of the 22 gauge and used for heavier items. Stem binding tape has two purposes (page 25): it gives an extra hold to wire stems and conceals the wire or green sticks (see below). Anchor tape is a strong adhesive tape used to secure foam and moss to containers (see opposite). Green canes are used for making stems longer. Candle holders are useful for holding candles firmly in place. They also make the replacement of candles easy to achieve. Wire-edged ribbon is considerably more expensive than ordinary ribbon but can be moulded into a variety of shapes that will hold.

Containers

Choosing your container is as important as selecting your flowers. Its size, shape and texture is important and will dictate to a certain extent the shape of the arrangement. As an approximate guide, the arrangement should be the twice the height again as the pot and twice the width.

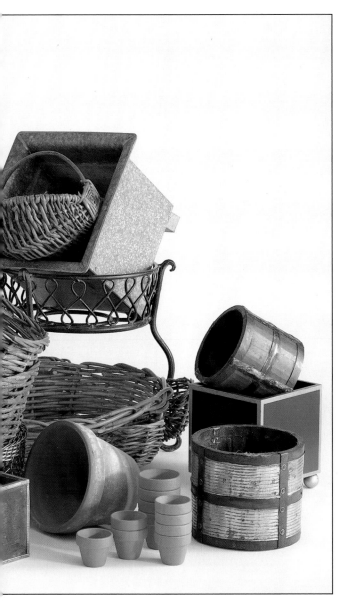

into the sides of the foam to soften the rim of the container. For narrow-necked containers, cut the foam a fraction bigger than the neck width and push into the pot. The foam should also have two-thirds of its length inside the container. When arranging, push wire stems all the way down through the foam and do not remove and insert stems too often, since the foam will disintegrate. Glass containers must first be filled, for example with pot pourri, moss, pebbles, nuts, shells, beans, pasta, fabric or paper, to conceal the foam. If using paper or fabric, line container first, then add a piece of foam 2.5 cm (1 in) smaller than the pot. Otherwise, place the foam in the container and fill around the edge. Cover with moss and tape in place. For a basket, fill with a piece of foam slightly bigger than the container. Trim the corners and cover with moss. Cut a piece of wire netting about 2.5 cm (1 in) smaller than the basket. Position on top of moss and attach to basket by threading black reel wire through the basket rim and netting, and twisting wire ends together. Repeat at intervals around the basket rim.

Covering a footed bowl

Spread out a piece of fabric right side down and place the pot in the centre. From underneath, gather up the fabric around the bowl's 'neck' and hold in place with one hand. Turn the bowl upside down and secure fabric to neck with a 22 gauge wire. Holding pot around neck, pull fabric downwards

gently to make even gathers all the way round. Now turn upright again and tuck excess fabric into the top of the pot.

Pinning moss to foam

Make pins from 18 or 22 gauge stem wire by cutting into 7.5-10 cm (3-4 in) lengths and bending in half. Use to pin plastic backing to moss (page 20) and moss or strings of chillies to foam.

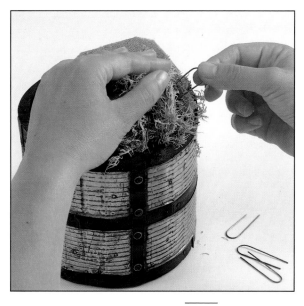

Dry foam fillings

Shallow bowls, flat dishes or plastic trays are tightly filled with foam to a higher level than the pot rim. Cover with a little sphagnum moss and secure in place with adhesive tape. A piece of foam can be glued inside a footed bowl with strong adhesive when tape or wire (see below) would show, but the container could not then be used for another purpose. Trim the corners of the foam to fit and make sure it sits at least 2.5 cm (1 in) above the pot rim. This enables stems to be inserted diagonally

Techniques

Ribbon bows

Single bow with tails: *Make a loop in the ribbon on either side of your thumb and forefinger leaving a similar length of hanging ribbon on either side as tails. Cut ribbon and twist one end of a 22 gauge stem wire around the middle.*

Double-looped bow: *As above except make 2 loops either side instead of one. To finish bow, cut a small length of ribbon and tie around the middle to cover the wire. Trim off excess ribbon at the bow back.*

Single loop without tails: *As single bow but do not make tails. Tuck the short ribbon ends into the loops and wire as before.*

Fabric bows

Cut a strip of fabric four times the required width and fold in half lengthways. Fold in half again, bringing the raw long edges to meet the fold, and glue. Cut the short ends diagonally, turn under the raw edges and glue. Make a bow with or without tails. To make the 'knot', cut a narrow length of fabric and with the reverse facing, fold the raw long edges into the middle, overlap and glue. Tie around the middle of the bow and cut off excess, or use this to form tails. Use the glue sparingly so that it does not seep through the fabric.

Moss-covered bases

Moss rope: *Cut a strip of wire netting 20 cm (8 in) wide. Fill with sphagnum moss, packing tightly since the tube needs to be quite solid. Wrap the netting around the moss and twist the cut wire ends around the netting to secure.*

Backing dry foam block: *Place moss and wire covered block face down. Cut a piece of double thickness black plastic a little larger than the block. Place over the base of the block and pin to the sides with wire pins made from 18 gauge wires cut into short lengths and bent in half. The plastic should not overlap the base onto the sides by more than 1.2 cm (½ in). The backing protects any surface upon which the block may be placed.*

Dry foam block: *Cut a piece of wire netting roughly twice the size of the block(s). Line the netting with a thin layer of moss and wrap around the block. Along the length of the block, twist the cut wire ends around the netting to secure. Cut away the excess netting at the sides of the block and twist the cut ends onto the netting as before.*

Cutting stems

To cut Eucalyptus, hold the leaves back and cut as close as possible to the next set of leaves. Repeat all the way down the stem until the latter begins to thicken. This procedure allows the maxiumum use of the stem. With multi-branched stems, cut undivided heads for use as they are, or small sprigs with 5-cm (2-in) stems to be wired for use in headdresses and small garlands. Stems 12.5-15 cm (5-6 in) in length are suitable for standard arrangements.

Bay leaf ball

Select several medium-sized fresh bay leaves and a medium-sized dry foam ball. Glue leaves to the ball using transparent-drying adhesive, beginning in the middle, generously overlapping the leaves. Slot other leaves behind and cover the ball completely. The leaves will shrink when they dry, so it is important to overlap them sufficiently.

Wiring a terracotta pot

Place a small piece of dry foam into a pot so that it fits snugly. Thread an 18 gauge wire through the bottom of the pot and between the foam and the side of the pot. The pot can then be wired onto a basket, moss rope or wreath.

Wiring a wreath

Cover an 18 gauge wire with stem binding tape and wrap around a wreath once only. Twist the ends of the wire tightly, so that the wire cannot move around the ring. Leave the ends of the wire apart so that they can be twisted onto a hook, around a curtain rail or whatever the wreath will be hung from. If the wreath is very thick and one wire is not long enough, twist two wires together and cover with stem binding tape.

Mounting candles

If using chunky beeswax candles, simply insert 2 or three pieces of cane into the bottom of the candle by not more than 2.5 cm (1 in). Attach legs to other thick candles by cutting 10-cm (4-in) pieces of cane. Hold one piece against the side of the candle and bind onto the candle with green adhesive tape. Then add the next 'leg' and bind as before. When all legs are in place, bind all together a few more times to secure. Legs can be attached to narrow candles, but candle holders are more practical.

Wiring stems

When decorating with or arranging dried flowers, it is best to attach the flowers, seedheads etc - either singly or in bunches - to lengths of wire, since their own stems are often too thick or brittle. Wiring also helps to create a more solid arrangement, as opposed to an airy, wispy effect. You will need 18 or 22 gauge stem wires, the 18 gauge being the strongest and used if the wire is to be the only support for the bunch. The 22 gauge wire is suitable for mounting bunches onto canes, used to create tall stems.

Take a bunch of dried material and cut stems to the required length - usually 12.5-17.5 cm (5-7 in). Hold stems together tightly at the bottom between thumb and forefinger. Bend a wire about two-thirds of the way along its length to from a loop. Place the loop under the bunch and hold in place with the third finger. Firmly twist the longer portion of the wire 5 or 6 times around the bunch, but not too tightly as to break the stems. To mount onto a cane, repeat the process but hold the cane under the bunch as you wire. Cinnamon sticks are available in a variety of sizes. Roll a bunch together in the hand to make them fit together. Hold the bunch tightly, place a wire around the middle and twist the ends together several times. The wire should be tight enough to cut into the bark slightly.

Nuts, pomegranates, cones, artichokes and single flowerheads

To wire a walnut, dip the end of a 22 gauge wire into latex-based adhesive, then push into the nut base where the two halves join. Leave to dry. Pomegranates are available loose, which can be glued onto 18 gauge wires, or ready glued to stems. They can also be wired onto canes. Small and medium-sized cones are wired with 22 gauge wires; larger cones require 18 gauge wires. Very large cones can be wired onto bamboo canes with 18 gauge wire. Loop a wire around the cone close to the base. Twist the ends together tightly. Trim the stems of artichokes to 2.5 cm (1 in) in length. Wind the wire through the leaves at the base, as for the cone, and twist the ends around the stem. Single flowers, such as roses, are wired in the same way as bunches.

Headdresses and small garlands

Use silver wires since they are fine but firm enough to take the weight of small flowers. Silver wire comes in 2 thicknesses – the thicker is best. Cut flowers from stems, either singly or in bunches. Hold firmly between thumb and forefinger. Make a loop in a length of wire and hold under the short stem. Wind one end around the length of stem about 6 times keeping the wire taut.

Binding stems

Tightly wind stem binding tape twice around the top of a wired stem or bunch to cover the wire. Hold firmly between thumb and forefinger and with the other hand, pull the tape downwards so that it stretches. Turn the stem between thumb and fore-finger while continuing to pull the tape downwards so that it twists around the length of wire. Body heat causes tape to stick to itself. Keep stretching for good adhesion and a thin covering.

Circlet

Overlap two 18 gauge wires by at least 10 cm (4 in). Twist a silver wire around the thicker wire, beginning at the top. Bind the entire length of wire with stem binding tape. Bend one end of the wire into a loop and bind in place with the tape. Bend the other end into a hook.

Bridesmaid's posy handle

Leaving a free length of ribbon 25 cm (10 in) in length, hold ribbon to the top of the handle and run the remainder of the ribbon downwards over the bottom of the handle, then upwards to the top of the handle. Hold both parts of the ribbon together with one hand. With the other hand, wrap the uncut ribbon down the handle. At this stage, the ribbon should be wrong side facing. At the bottom of the handle, fold over the excess ribbon and wrap with the ribbon, which should be twisted so that the right side is now facing. Work upwards to the handle top and tie the ribbon onto the free length. Make a simple bow and tie to the top of the handle with a double knot. Insert a long pearl-ended pin into the centre of the bow and push up through the posy.

Using bung moss

Use a pair of florist's scissors to trim away the root portion of the bung moss before use. This enables the moss to fit smoothly onto a surface as well as making it easier to glue.

To make a topiary

1 *Fill a pot three-quarters full with nylon-reinforced plaster or quick-drying plaster. The former is cleaner and heavier. If using the latter, first place some stones in the bottom of the pot. This kind of plaster will harden in a few minutes, while the reinforced type will take up to 24 hours to dry. Set the main trunk in the centre of the pot, then branches around the trunk, if desired. Wire the branches to the trunk at the bottom and top. Cut a hole the same circumference as the trunk and approximately 5 cm (2 in) deep in a dry foam ball. Cut a piece of wire netting large enough to cover the ball. Wrap around the ball keeping the hole clear of wire.*

2 *Squeeze some glue from a glue gun into the hole and push the ball onto the trunk. Leave to dry. Thread a 22 gauge wire through the netting at the ball base and around the trunk. Twist the ends tightly to secure. Repeat at equal intervals around the trunk.*

3 *Push wired items or stems into the ball beginning at the middle top. Work around and down, keeping the dried materials very close together.*

4 *To create a different-shaped topiary, select dry foam blocks to give the required size. Glue blocks together using a glue gun. When dry, cut the foam to a desired shape. A slightly oval shape is effective for a moss topiary. Treat in the same way as the foam ball.*

Decorative Gifts

Surprise and delight your family and friends by making stylish and individual dried flower gifts especially for them. Here is a range of inspirational ideas, from exquisitely-packaged pot pourri to a rustic wreath of culinary herbs, both practical and decorative. Alternatively, enhance any gift package with an elegant dried flower decoration.

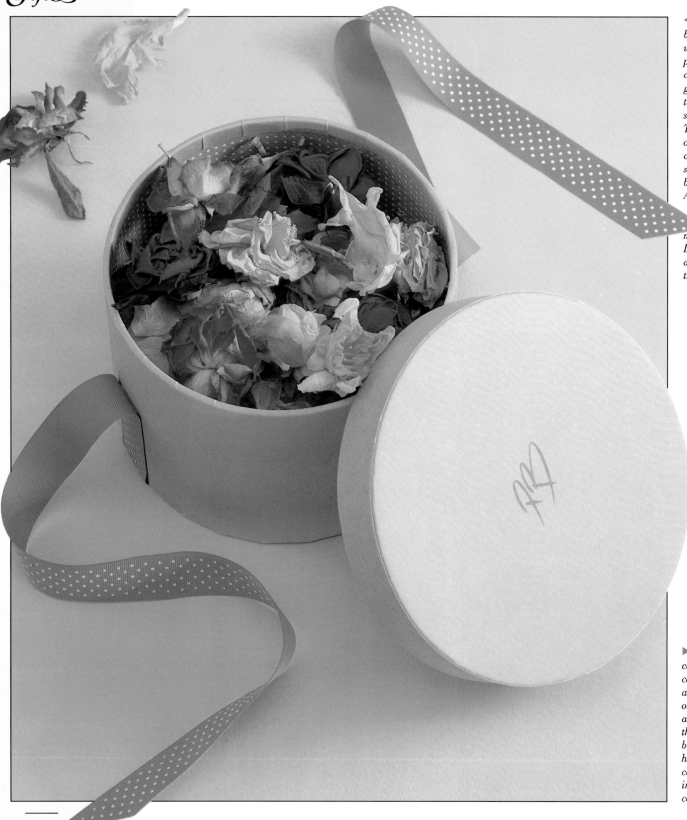

◀ *Decorate a brightly-coloured box with matching ribbon and fill with a fragrant and eye-catching pot pourri mixture – perhaps consisting of flowers and herbs gathered from your garden throughout the spring and summer. We chose yellow ('Golden Times'), red ('Jaguar') and orange ('Tennessee') roses; daffodil heads and pumpkin seeds. Place your ingredients in a bowl and mix to evenly disperse. Add a few drops of rose essential oil or another oil of your choice drop by drop. Transfer mixture to a plastic bag and seal. Leave in a dark, cool place for about 6 weeks. Shake the bag thoroughly twice a week.*

▶ *Gift packages for any occasion can be transformed from the commonplace with the simple addition of dried flowerheads and other material. Keep the glue gun away from the parcel when gluing the flowers and be careful not to burn your fingers when applying hot glue to small dried items. You can use a strong, tube adhesive instead, but avoid any direct contact with the fingers.*

1 *Wrap parcels and decorate with ribbon. Draw outlines of the designs in pencil onto the parcels.*

2 *Using a glue gun, apply glue to the bottom of each flower and position.*

3 *Glue on nuts and fruits one at a time.*

◀ *Napkins can be effectively decorated for a celebration table using wire-edged ribbon, which can be arranged to create attractive shapes, flowerheads, cones or seedheads. Choose colours and textures to ccordinate with the overall colour scheme or theme of the table.*

▶ *A dainty and delightful basket arrangement that would make an elegant addition to a treasured friend or relative's beside or dressing table.*

You will need:
2 bunches lavender
1 bunch red roses
1 bunch marjoram
1 bunch Eucalyptus
1 bunch orange Helichrysum
7 open orange roses
Wire roses, Helichrysum *and* Eucalyptus *in groups of three stems, but marjoram and lavender in small bunches. Use 22 gauge wire and bind with tape (pages 24-25).*

1 *Cut block of oasis to fit snugly in basket. Cover lightly with moss and wire netting.*

2 *Position bunches of either lavender or marjoram to create the basic shape.*

3 *At the front of the basket, gently bend the bunches downwards to cover the edge.*

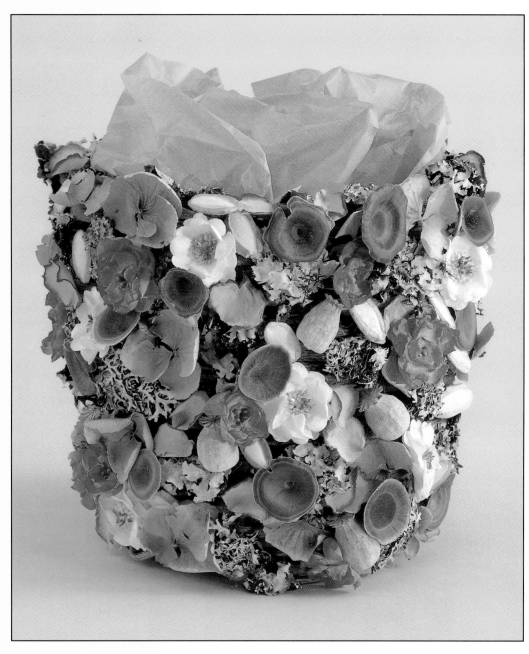

◄ *Turn an ordinary wicker basket into an original and highly attractive gift by decorating the outside with a colourful variety of dried and artificial items. For this design, we used tree mushrooms, white paper flowers, tree lychin moss, small poppy seedheads, florets of artificial hydrangea and petals of a 'Minuet' rose. Simply apply glue from a glue gun to the bottom of each item and position on the basket.*

► *This inviting herbal wreath makes the ideal gift for any cook. It will bring natural fragrance to the kitchen as well as a ready supply of herbs for culinary purposes.*

You will need:
A twig ring
1 bunch fresh rosemary
1 bunch marjoram
5 bushy stems fresh bay
70 dried chillies
Trim stems of marjoram and rosemary to 17.5 cm (7 in) in length; bay leaves can be shorter.

1 *Attach a wire to hang the wreath (page 23). Using silver reel wire, wire together bunches of chillies, then wire with 22 gauge stem wires and bind with stem binding tape (pages 24-25).*

2 *Wire a bunch of marjoram to ring.*

3 *Add chillies, bay then rosemary. Repeat pattern until wreath is complete.*

Weddings

Dried flowers offer a highly practical and versatile alternative to fresh flowers for weddings. Obviously their use avoids altogether the major problem of wilting on a hot day. Vibrantly-coloured dried material can be combined to create dramatic headdresses, corsages and posies, which can all be made well in advance of the big day.

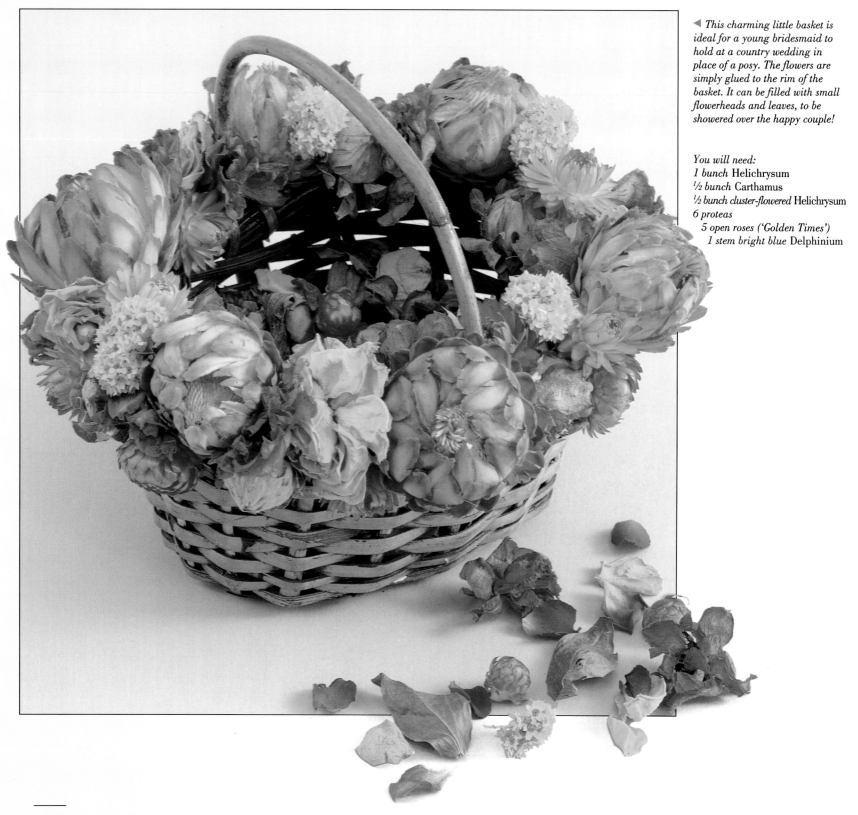

◀ *This charming little basket is ideal for a young bridesmaid to hold at a country wedding in place of a posy. The flowers are simply glued to the rim of the basket. It can be filled with small flowerheads and leaves, to be showered over the happy couple!*

You will need:
1 bunch Helichrysum
½ bunch Carthamus
½ bunch cluster-flowered Helichrysum
6 proteas
5 open roses ('Golden Times')
1 stem bright blue Delphinium

To make a bridesmaid's pomander, wrap a dry foam ball in a square of fabric, gather at the top and secure with a 22 gauge wire. Trim excess fabric to 10 cm (4 in) above wire. Fold over and tuck in rough fabric edges. Make a fabric ribbon and tie on. Glue flowerheads around the wire.

1 For the corsage, cover a 10-cm (4-in) piece of 18 gauge wire with stem binding tape (page 25). Wire and bind flowerheads and leaves (pages 24-25). Twist a wired leaf onto one end of a length of wire and bind with stem binding tape. Add a wired flower below and twist onto leaf wire.

2 Cover wire with stem binding tape. Continue adding flowers and bind with tape. Trim excess wires as you work.

▶ To make a more secure decoration for the pomander, wire flowers onto a wire ring following the instructions for the champagne bottle wreath on page 49, then attach to the pomander around the 'neck'. These dainty decorations are light and easy for junior bridesmaids to hold.

39

1 *Bind hoop tightly with ribbon.*

2 *Cut flowers from stems at the top and spread on a tray. Measure 10 cm (4 in) either side of the top middle point of hoop. Begin gluing small flowerheads to hoop.*

3 *Use larger flowers at the centre bottom for balance. Make two small bows (pages 20-21) and attach to hoop.*

▲ *This elegant hoop makes an unusual alternative to the more traditional posy. The bows can be omitted for a simpler, cleaner effect.*

▶ *Give your wedding gifts a chic personal touch by gluing dried flowers – either single heads or bunches – onto giftwrap or decorative ribbon. Here, we have used 2 peony heads and a small bunch of lavender with pale blue wire-edged ribbon for the white package; a glycerined mauve anemone (page 16) with gold ribbon for the blue/gold marbled box.*

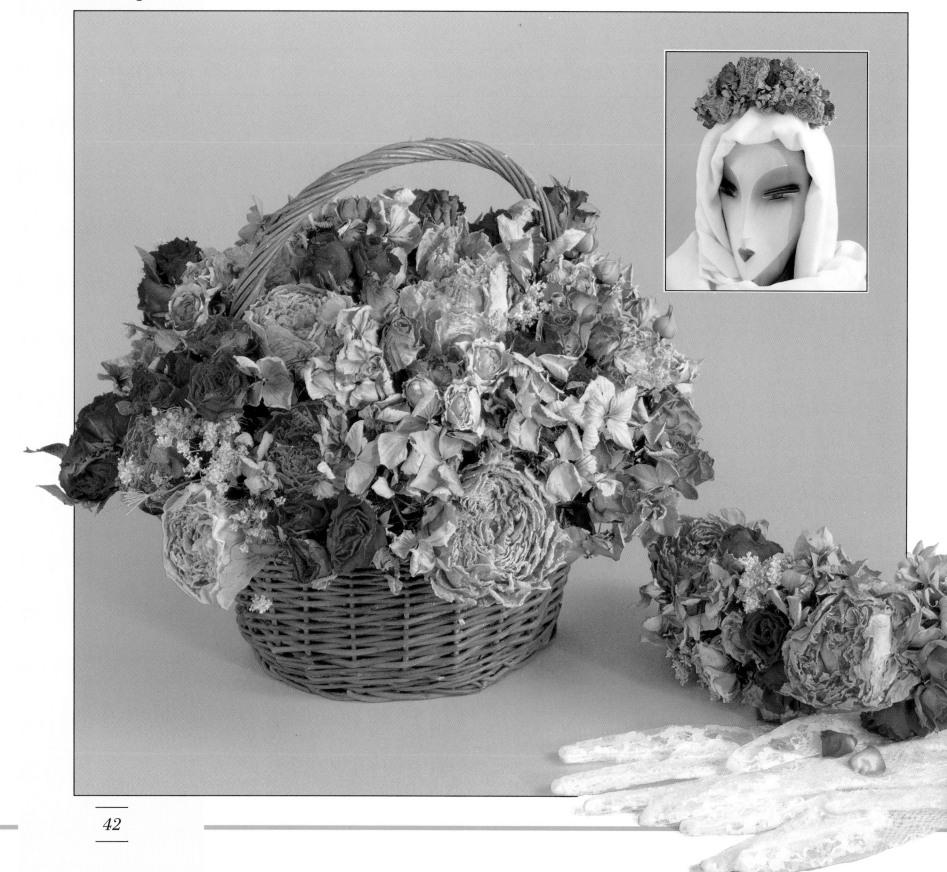

◀ *The frosted blue hydrangea and touches of cow parsley give a lacy quality to these decorative accessories. Follow the instructions on page 33 to make the basket, using the bunches of red roses to create the basic shape. To make the headdress, refer to the instructions on page 45.*

For both the basket and the headdress, you will need:
1 bunch cow parsley
40 stems dark red roses ('Jaguar')
10 stems miniature pink species roses ('Pink Delight')
10 peonies
2 heads hydrangea

1 *Begin with the bottom of the bouquet. Twist wired stems of flowers and leaves onto each other to form a soft, oval-shaped 'tail'. Continue to add stems until the tail is at least 25 cm (10 in) long. Bend the wire ends downwards to form a handle at least 15 cm (6 in) away from the flowers.*

2 *Make a light posy 20-25 cm (8-10 in) in diameter with silver reel wire, bind stem of posy to stem of 'tail' below handle. Hold the bouquet's handle in front of a mirror and add more flowers to fill any gaps. Trim excess wires and cut handle to hand size. Cover well with stem binding tape. Cover with ribbon and add bow (pages 26-27).*

For the bouquet, you will need:
30-40 stems poly-dried flowers
3 m (3⅓ yd) x 3-cm (1¼-in) wide ribbon
Wire flowerheads with 22 gauge wires (pages 24-25) – their original stems are far too heavy. Cover wire with stem binding tape (page 25) and group in jars or vases to make selection easier.

◀ *Poly-dried flowers are an effective artificial alternative to real dried flowers. Made from polyester, they are able to withstand considerable wear and tear. Make a headdress from poly-dried flowers to match the bouquet following the instructions on page 45.*

You will need:
2 bunches marjoram
2 bunches lavender
27 orange roses, one large
20 red roses
Wire roses singly; marjoram and
lavender in small bunches (pages
24-25) using 22 gauge wires.
Cover wire with stem binding tape
(page 25).

1 *Begin with the large rose in the
centre and surround with
marjoram. Bind the stems together
with silver reel wire where your
hand is holding the bouquet. Add
next set of flowers – about 5 stems
– and wire. Turn the posy as you
work.*

2 *Check side of posy occasionally
to make sure that you are creating
a domed shape. When complete,
trim wire stems and bind with
stem binding tape (page 25).
Cover handle with ribbon (pages
26-27).*

▶ *When making the posy, once you have covered stems with stem binding tape, place flowers in jars – the same type in one jar – for easy access and selection.*

For the headdress you will need:
6-8 thimble-sized terracotta pots
Tiny bunches of various dried flowers
Single flowerheads, eg roses, sunflowers and marigolds
15 x 7.5-cm (3-in) squares fabric
Wire tiny bunches and single flowerheads onto silver wires and cover with stem binding tape (page 25). Wire terracotta pots (page 23) and fill each with a wired flowerhead, the wire end fed through the hole in the pot bottom. Gather up corners of each fabric square and wire with silver wire. Bind with stem binding tape.

◀ *You will need to build up your confidence and competence before attempting this formal, Victorian-style posy, but your endeavours will be well rewarded.*

1 *Make a circlet (page 25). Begin at hook end and twist wired flowers etc onto circlet (page 49). Trim excess wires as you work. Finish 7.5 cm (3 in) from loop. Make a corsage (page 39) using same flowers as in first 10 cm (4 in) of circlet. Using a silver wire covered with stem binding tape (page 25), attach corsage in three places to circlet, the wire end of corsage tucking under flowers on circlet.*

2 *For posy, wire flowers with 22 gauge wires and cover with stem binding tape (pages 24-25). Take 5-8 stems and tightly bind together 12.5 cm (5 in) from the flowerheads (5-7.5 cm/2-3 in for small bridesmaids) using silver reel wire. Whilst turning stems in one hand, open them out to create a frame. Add other flowers, binding one stem in place at a time. Finally, trim wires, bind handle with tape and ribbon (pages 26-27).*

Valentines

Flowers are universally chosen to mark the great romantic
milestones - courtship; engagement; wedding and anniversary.
The versatility of dried flowers offers the opportunity to create a
wide variety of displays and decorations of lasting significance.

You will need:
2 bunches Ageratum
100 stems red roses
Wire rose heads singly with silver wires and cover with stem binding tape (page 25). Wire Ageratum into groups of 5 heads and bind.

1 *Use silver wire to join two 18 gauge wires together and bind with stem binding tape (page 25). Bend wire to form shape. Attach ends together by forming a loop and hook (page 25).*

2 *Twist flowers onto heart starting from the middle top and working outwards and downwards. Keep the flowers even all the way around.*

◀ A stunning heart-shaped wreath to adorn a wall or door at a wedding or anniversary reception. When wiring the flowers to the wreath, rest the heart on a work surface.

▶ A delightful decoration for a celebratory bottle of bubbly. It is important to select vividly-coloured flowers to contrast with the colour of the bottle. Lay flowers out on your work surface to see how they work together before wiring.

1 *Select a few small brightly-coloured flowers and bind with silver wires (page 25). Bind with stem binding tape (page 25).*

2 *Bend an 18 gauge wire into a hoop, overlap ends and twist together. Cover with stem binding tape. Bind flowers onto hoop one at a time, making 3 or 4 twists then trimming excess wire. Continue until hoop is full. To add last flower, pull other flowers away slightly, wire on flower and re-arrange others.*

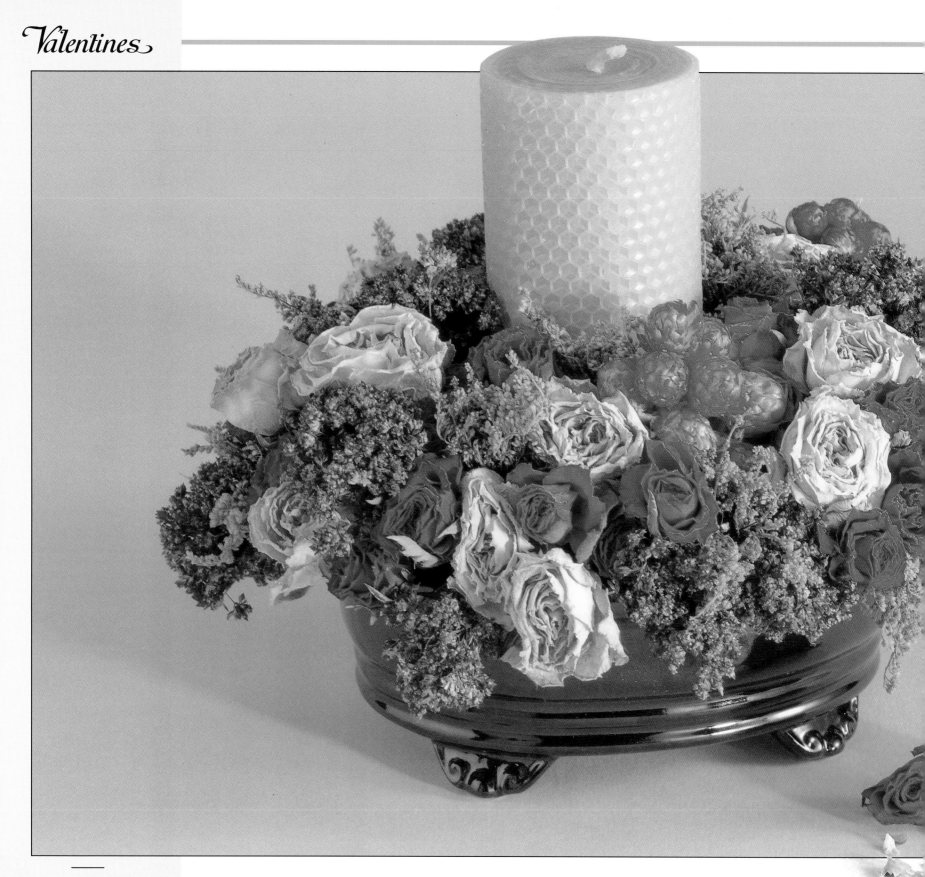

◀ *A rich arrangement to crown an intimate dining table or grace a dressing table. Refer to the instructions on page 103 to create the arrangement, using the bunches of marjoram to set the basic shape. But first position the beeswax candle in the centre of the foam by inserting short lengths of green cane into the bottom of the candle (page 23).*

You will need:
2 bunches marjoram
1 bunch globe amaranth
1 bunch green golden rod
20 red roses
15 open peach roses
A chunky beeswax candle

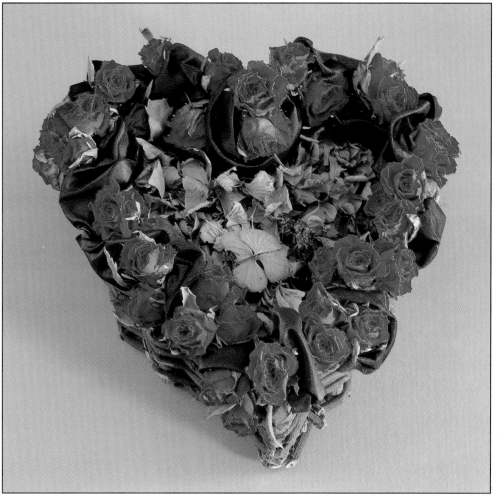

Line the basket with plastic, then cover with fabric. The plastic will prevent any essential oils from seeping through the basket onto the table.

1 *Glue ribbon onto basket. Squeeze a small amount of glue from a glue gun, wait a few seconds then press ribbon onto glue, thus avoiding any risk of burning your fingers.*

2 *Cut roses from stems entirely. Squeeze a little glue onto underside of each rose and hold in place on the basket until glue dries. When finished, remove any strands of glue. Fill basket with hydrangea florets and add a few drops of essential oil if desired.*

▲ *This sumptous heart-shaped basket filled with fragrant pot pourri will make a memorable engagement gift.*

You will need:
30-35 roses
2 heads hydrangea
2 m (2¼ yd) wire-edged ribbon

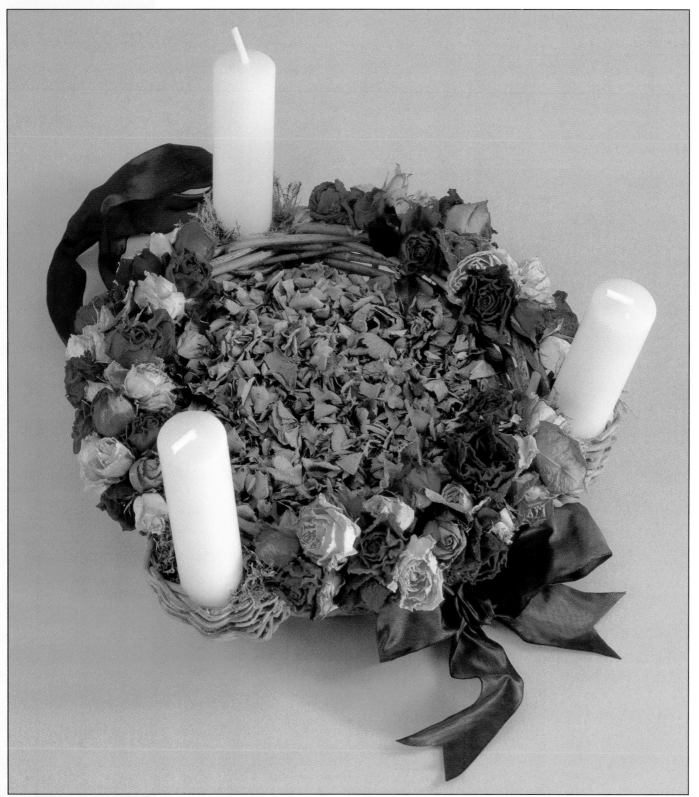

◀ *There are many different styles of basket available and they can all be decorated to great effect with dried flowers. You will enjoy looking out for new varieties to transform into eye-catching decorations for the home. Our wicker basket has holders for candles and has been decorated with assorted pink roses interspersed with a few rose leaves.*

▶ *This is a facing arrangement, ie it is designed to be viewed from the front or sides; it is not an all-round arrangement. This is an extravagant display for a very special occasion, to stand in an empty fireplace or against a wall.*

You will need:
5 bunches cones
4 bunches peach roses
3-5 bunches marjoram
3 bunches assorted roses
2 bunches mixed species roses
2 bunches green golden rod
15 cinnamon sticks
7 heads hydrangea
5 stems artificial fruits
1 m (1⅛ yd) silk

Fill pot with dry foam, making sure it fits securely. Cover lightly with moss and tape in place.

1 Cut the silk into nine squares. Gather up corners, hold tightly together and bind with silver wire. Wire each gathered fabric piece onto a green cane using 22 gauge wire (pages 24-25). Tuck in any rough edges. Bind with stem binding tape. Wire bunches of flowers, fruits, cones and cinnamon sticks onto canes and bind (pages 24-25).

2 Begin at back of pot and place first bunch of flowers three-quarters of the way back from front of pot. Place bunches around outer edge and middle of arrangement to make a basic frame in which to work. Fill in with other canes pushing some deeper into the foam to give dimension.

53

1 Push pole into plaster. Trim leaves from rose stems and place around pole. Push stems into plaster and wire to pole at top.

2 Cut a small hole in foam ball (page 26), fill with glue and push onto pole. Leave to set.

3 Push roses into ball starting at the top. Tie ribbon around poles and cover plaster with moss.

◄ *This pair of elegant rose topiaries would make an unusual mantelpiece display for a social gathering to celebrate a special anniversary.*

You will need:
2 birch poles 2.5-3.75cm (1-1½ in)
   in diameter, 30cm (12 in) in
   length
200 roses
A little moss
1 m (1⅛ yd) ribbon
Line two pots with plastic and fill a half to three-quarters full with nylon-reinforced plaster (page 26). Cut roses from stems leaving 2.5 cm (1 in) of stem on flowers. Do not discard stems.

▶ *In this opulent arrangement, bunches of crimson, deep pink, pale pink and pale yellow roses are packed closely together to form a solid domed shape, broken at intervals with contrasting sprigs of blue/green Eucalyptus (pages 22-23).*

Valentines

You will need:
2 bunches marjoram
40 roses
1 m (1⅛ yd) ribbon
Roses must be stripped of leaves
and thorns to about three-quarters
of the way up stems.

1 *Separate stems of dried material*
so they can be picked up easily with
one hand. Hold a small bunch of
stems in one hand, then add one
stem at a time, spiralling the stems
as you go. Flowers should get
shorter around outer edge.

2 *Bind stems together with wire*
or stem binding tape. Cover with
ribbon and a bow (pages 20-21).
Trim stems so posy can stand.

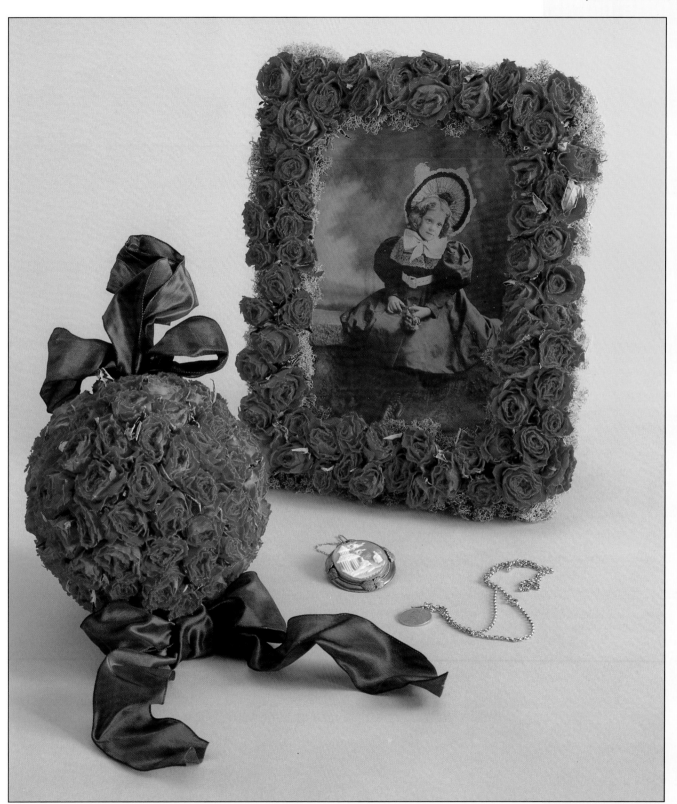

◄ *A posy with a difference - the stems are twisted so that they splay, enabling it to stand upright. A dramatic centrepiece for a large-scale celebration dining or buffet table.*

▶ *These are romantic gifts or decorations with a distinctively Victorian feel. Follow the instructions on page 58 to make the pomander. Make a bow (pages 20-21) and push wire stems into the bottom of the ball. Wire a loop of fabric and insert into the ball top to hang. A plain wooden picture frame can be enhanced by gluing on lychin moss and rose heads.*

1 *Select size of foam ball required. Trim rose stems to 2.5 cm (1 in) in length.*

2 *Hold ball in palm of the hand. Push roses into foam close together.*

3 *Complete one side of ball, turn over and gently continue inserting roses into ball until covered entirely.*

◄ *Even the smallest size of foam ball requires a great many roses to fully cover it. However, if you wanted to group a few rose balls in a bowl, you could leave the foam bare where it was not visible, to use fewer roses. Drape ribbon or fabric around the balls to conceal any bare patches.*

You will need:
7.5-12.5 cm (3-5 in) dry foam balls
100 roses (for 10 cm/4 in balls)

▲ *Delight a loved one or a bride to be with a collection of pretty and fragrant homemade pomanders. Cut a square or circular piece of muslin and fill with lavender or a pot pourri (page 30). Gather the edges of the muslin together and tie with narrow string. Trim excess muslin if necessary. Place the bag upright in the centre of a piece of fabric. Gather up the edges around the bag and fasten at the 'neck' with silver reel wire. Cover with coordinating ribbon and tie the end in a loop. Tuck the raw edges of the fabric down into the neck of the bag, arranging the fabric into attractive folds.*

59

◀ *These miniature terracotta pot arrangements would make unusual table decorations for a celebration of romance. Fill the pots tightly with foam and insert trimmed rose stems, small bunches of marjoram or lavender. Push a short length of green cane into the bottom of the candle (page 23) and insert into the foam.*

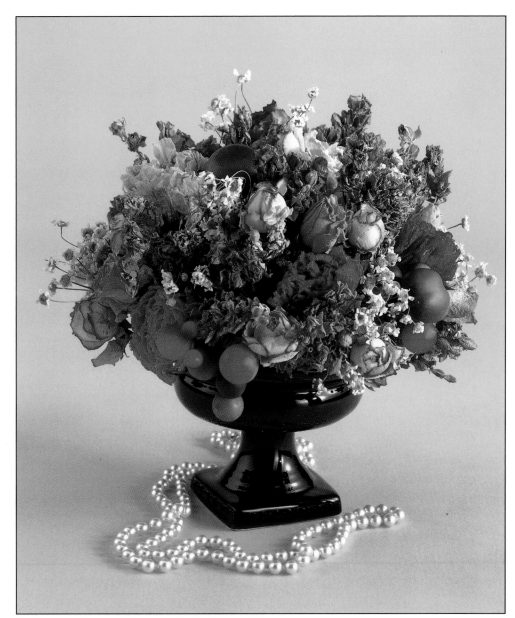

▶ *A subtle but beautiful miniature arrangement. Bend the bunches at the front forwards over the edge of the pot to create a softer effect. When arranging, stand back from the arrangement at intervals to check the overall shape.*

You will need:
2 bunches blue larkspur
1 bunch chamomile daisy
20 assorted roses
5 pink peonies
5 dark purple peonies
1 stem artificial fruits

1 *Push a slightly over-sized block of foam into pot. Trim corners, cover lightly with moss and tape in place.*

2 *Wire flowers in small bunches with 22 gauge wires (pages 24-25) to make 7.5 cm (3 in) stems and bind with stem binding tape (page 25). There is no need to wire peonies.*

3 *Cut fruit from stem, wire and bind as above. Start with peonies then add other flowers.*

Spring

Herald the awakening of spring by creating a unique decoration or display for the home that exploits woodland textures and natural colours bringing with it a feeling of re-birth and rejuvenation. Here we present novel ideas for gifts, arrangements for Eastertide as well as table centrepieces.

Lay a thick layer of moss over the tray or board and bind in place with black reel wire. Complete one side, then turn over and cover the other side.

1 *To make bunny, tightly bind a handful of moss. Add more moss and bind until the body is complete. Make ears and tail in the same way and bind onto body. Use the berries for eyes and nose.*

2 *Cut several 18 gauge wires into three pieces and bend each into a hairpin shape. Use to pin bunny to tray or board.*

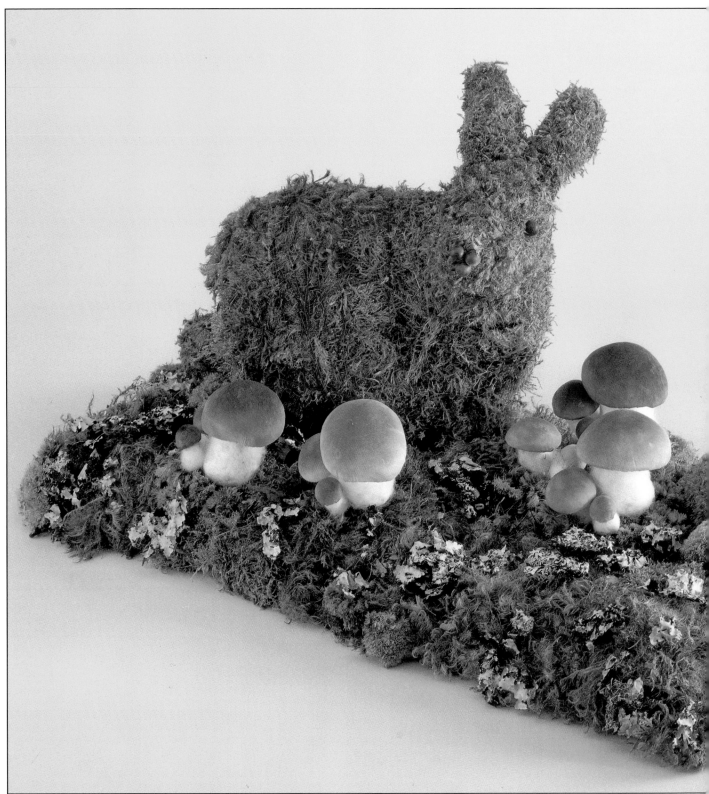

◀ *A country bunny decoration makes an appropriate centrepiece for Easter. If you intend to move him around, glue the bung and lychin moss to the sphagnum moss.*

You will need:
A rectangular piece of wood or standard-sized tray
Sphagnum moss, fresh
Bung and lychin moss
Artificial mushrooms
1 stem artificial berries

▲ *Present a gift of fresh, potted herbs or other plants in a woodland-inspired box. Select a sturdy fruit or moss box and bind sphagnum moss to the sides with black reel wire. Line box with thick plastic or a plant tray.*

Thread twigs through the wire on the box sides. and insert flower stems into the moss to add colour.

1 *Place bung moss into a vase then some pebbles to fill one-third. Add a block of dry foam. Add more moss and pebbles.*

2 *Wire cinnamon sticks and other drieds (pages 24-25). Bind with stem binding tape (page 25). Make holes in sea sponges for wiring.*

3 *Push wire through the holes and twist. Position sea sponge, then other material. Add soaked and squeezed moss.*

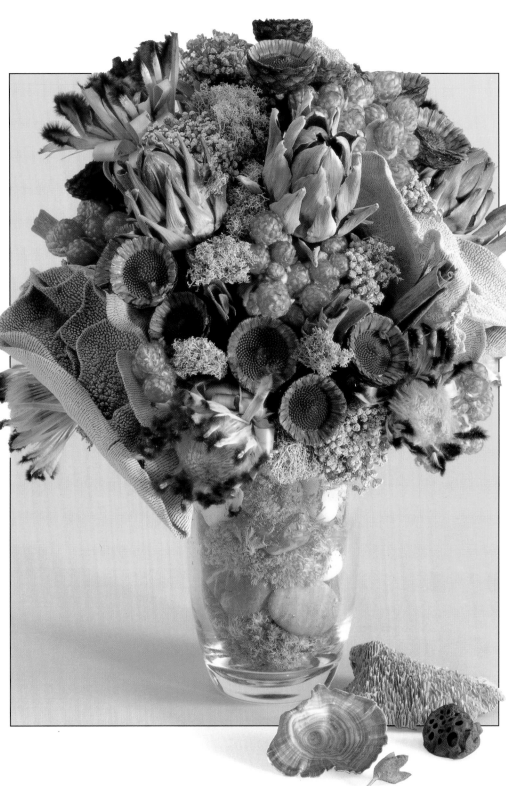

You will need:
2 bunches globe amaranth
18 stems Anaphalis (pearl everlasting)
15 stems cones
10 cinnamon sticks
9 proteas
6 artichoke heads
3 large sea sponges
Ground lychin and bung moss
Pebbles

◀ *The lychin moss should be soaked in warm water and squeezed as dry as possible before being used in the arrangement. It will dry in place, so there is no need to wire.*

▶ *Stripped branches of contorted willow can be presented in an interesting container to create a minimalistic yet atmospheric display. The shape of the arrangement can be changed from time to time for added interest – from windswept to a wide and shallow dome or triangle.*

1 Attach wire to ring for hanging (page 23). Place ring on a well-protected surface. Trim root base from moss (page 26).

2 Squeeze a small amount of glue onto underside of moss. Position clumps close together on ring – hold in position until set.

3 Leave 2.5 cm (1 in) of bare ring for a ribbon bow (pages 20-21). Glue on button chrysanthemums in between moss clumps.

You will need:
A dry foam ring
Bung moss
Button chrysanthemums

▲ An attractive ring that brings the suggestion of fresh spring grass into the home.

1 *Cover underside of ring in fabric. Glue to sides of ring to a level of 1 cm (½ in).*

2 *Apply glue to the reverse of the fabric and press in place. Be very careful not to burn your fingers.*

3 *Wire flowers and cover with stem binding tape (pages 24-25). Trim wires so that they do not pierce underside of wreath when mounted.*

You will need:
A foam ring 30 cm (12 in) in diameter
3 bunches grasses
1 bunch blue larkspur

1 bunch Alchemilla
20 stems roses
20 tree mushrooms
6 artificial mushrooms
3 heads hydrangea

Wire roses, larkspur and Alchemilla in small bunches; wire cinnamon sticks in pairs and pomegranates (pages 24-25). Trim stems of peonies – there is no need to wire.

1 *Make a 7.5-cm (3-in) moss rope (page 21). Wire to rim of basket. Cut a foam block into eighths. Cover pieces in moss and wire netting (page 21). Wire at intervals to rope. Fill pots with foam and wire up (page 23). Attach to moss rope close to blocks.*

2 *Drape fabric between blocks and secure in place with 22 gauge wires. Fill blocks and pots with dried material. Tie decorative paper rope at intervals around the fabric swags.*

▲ *You will need:*
6 mini terracotta pots
2 bunches Alchemilla
1 bunch blue larkspur
40 yellow roses
12 dark purple peonies
10 pomegranates
Large bag cinnamon sticks
Sphagnum moss
1 m (1⅛ yd) narrow rope
1 m (1⅛ yd) blue silk

▶ *You will need:*
3 bunches glycerined Eucalyptus
3 bunches cat mint
80 peach roses
15 pomegranates
Sphagnum moss
3 candles
2 m (2¼ yd) white muslin
Wire flowers and foliage in bunches with 22 gauge wires and cover with stem binding tape (pages 24-25). Wire pomegranates with 18 gauge wires (pages 24-25).

1 *Place muslin inside container and drape heavily around sides but keep flat on bottom. Place foam on top and cover with moss.*

2 *Cut green canes into 10 cm (4 in) pieces. Tape cane pieces to bottom of candles (page 23). Group candles centrally.*

3 *Position dried material leaving at least 7.5 cm (3 in) of candle visible.*

1 *Cut a dry foam block in half, trim and push into container; make sure it fits tightly. Cover with moss and tape in place.*

2 *Position 8 bunches – 2-3 in the centre and the remainder around edge – to create the arrangement's basic shape.*

3 *Intersperse hydrangea heads making them slightly shorter than the other bunches. Add remainder of flowers.*

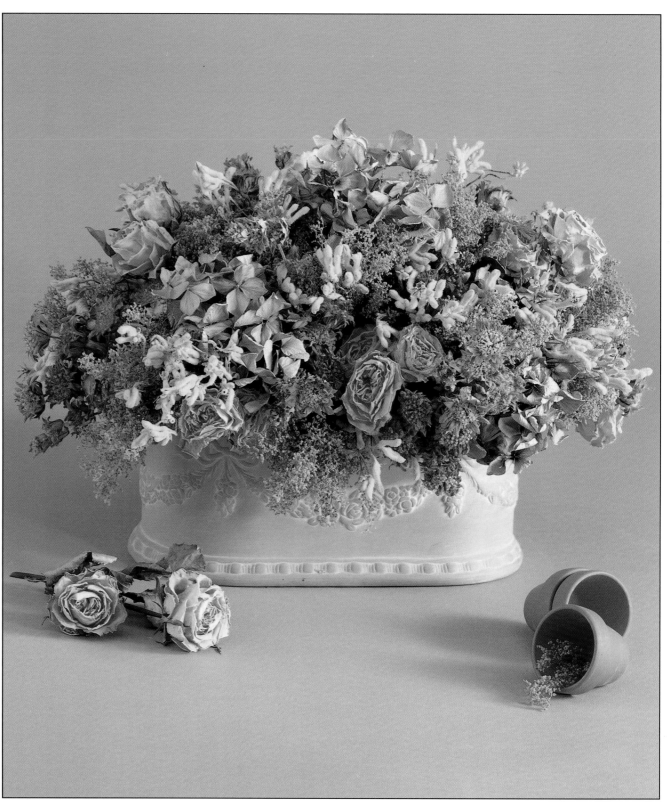

◀ *Dimension is added to this arrangement by lowering the height of the hydrangea heads in relation to the other flowers.*

You will need:
2 bunches Ambrosinia
2 bunches scabious
20 stems large headed roses
8 stems yellow kangaroo paws
4 heads hydrangea
Wire bunches of flowers with 22 gauge stem wires and cover with stem binding tape (pages 24-25).

▶ *A pastel-shaded arrangement for a side or occasional table. Fill a glass container with sphagnum moss, then place a piece of foam on top and tape in place. Follow the instructions on page 61, but aim for a more solid, domed shape.*

You will need:
3 bunches artificial berries
2 bunches lavender
1 bunch Achillea
1 bunch marjoram
30 stems peach roses ('Gerdo')
3 heads hydrangea

Summer

Summertime offers a profusion of beautiful blooms for drying and combining to create stunning arrangements. Make an empty fireplace a focal point with a dramatic firescreen, or decorate a plain wall with a posy of pickings. Alternatively, bring a breath of summer into a tired winter interior with a rustic pot of sunflowers or a pair of dazzling yellow topiaries.

1 *Round off corners of wood by drawing around a plate. Cut along pencil line with a saw.*

2 *Place wood on fabric and trim excess leaving a 5 cm (2 in) border. Fold border over screen edge and pin or glue.*

3 *Encase cord in a 7.5-cm (3-in) wide fabric strip the length of screen's perimeter. Glue rough edges of piping to screen back and piping to screen front.*

◀ *This firescreen is easily decorated with a variety of colourful flowerheads and artificial fruits – simply glue them to the fabric. The fabric strip for the piping can be made from short strips of fabric sewn together end to end to form one long strip.*

You will need:
A piece of plywood approximately 60 x 45 cm (2 x 1½ ft)
Assorted dried flowerheads and artificial fruits
2 m (2⅔ yd) heavy green fabric
3 m (3⅓ yd) x 3.75 cm (1½ in) wide thick cord

▶ *This is a facing, flat-backed arrangement to be viewed from the front and sides only. It is therefore an ideal arrangement to fill the gaping hole of an empty fireplace during the summer months. Soften the front of the display by bending the flowers forwards over the edge of the container.*

You will need:
4 bunches cream zinnias
4 bunches Ambrosinia
4 bunches assorted roses
3 bunches globe thistles (Echinops)
2 bunches sunflowers
14 small heads hydrangea

Wire about a third of flowers onto green canes and cover with stem binding tape (pages 24-25). Wire remainder with 18 gauge wires and bind with tape.

1 *Push foam into container to fit tightly leaving 10 cm (4 in) visible above pot rim. Cover with moss.*

2 *Create the basic shape with some of the taller items at back and shorter flowers around edge.*

3 *To judge the required length of an item on a green cane, measure it against pot before trimming. Position remaining flowers.*

1 Cut the stems of Eucalyptus *into* short lengths taking care to cut the stems as close as possible to the next set of leaves. This enables the whole stem to be used, not just the top.

2 Wire bunches of 3 Eucalyptus pieces tightly together with 22 gauge wire. Cut off excess wire to leave a clear 5 cm (2 in) of stem. Make the topiary base (page 26) with the branches and either a foam ball or oval shape. Push the Eucalyptus bunches into the foam as close together as posible. Cover the quick-drying plaster with a little moss.

◀ *An unusual foliage topiary. Eucalpytus is attractive both for its silver blue-green colour and its interesting leaf formation.*

You will need:
3 branches 2.5 cm (1 in) in
*   diameter, 25 cm (10 in) in length*
8 bunches glycerined Eucalyptus
A little bung or lychin moss

▶ *A pot full of zest! Fill a terracotta pot with foam and cover lightly with moss. Tape or pin in place (page 19). Wire bunches of Solidago, Celosia and button chrysanthemums with 22 gauge stem wires and bind with stem binding tape (pages 24-25). The remaining flowers can be left on their original stems.*

You will need:
2 bunches Celosia
2 bunches yellow button
* chrysanthemums*
* 2 bunches Solidago*
* 10 red roses ('Jaguar')*
* 6 dark pink peonies*
* 6 sunflowers*
* 4 zinnias*
* 2 m (2¼ yd) wire-edged*
*   green ribbon*

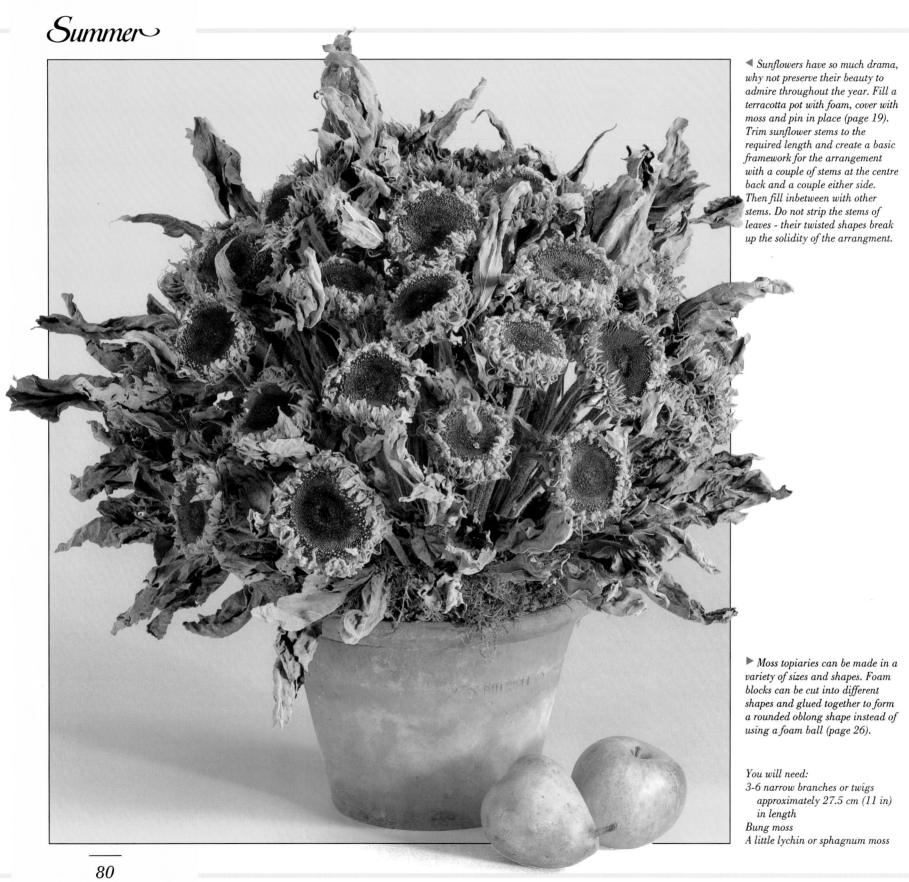

◀ Sunflowers have so much drama, why not preserve their beauty to admire throughout the year. Fill a terracotta pot with foam, cover with moss and pin in place (page 19). Trim sunflower stems to the required length and create a basic framework for the arrangement with a couple of stems at the centre back and a couple either side. Then fill inbetween with other stems. Do not strip the stems of leaves - their twisted shapes break up the solidity of the arrangment.

▶ Moss topiaries can be made in a variety of sizes and shapes. Foam blocks can be cut into different shapes and glued together to form a rounded oblong shape instead of using a foam ball (page 26).

You will need:
3-6 narrow branches or twigs
    approximately 27.5 cm (11 in)
    in length
Bung moss
A little lychin or sphagnum moss

1 *Make a topiary base (page 26) – the branches should extend 20 cm (8 in) above pot rim. Attach foam ball.*

2 *Trim off the root part of the bung moss clumps (page 26).*

3 *Squeeze glue from a glue gun onto underside of moss. Place clumps onto foam as close together as possible. Keep fingers away from hot glue. Cover cement with moss.*

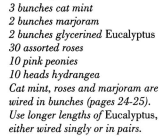

◀ *You will need:*
3 bunches cat mint
2 bunches marjoram
2 bunches glycerined Eucalyptus
30 assorted roses
10 pink peonies
10 heads hydrangea
Cat mint, roses and marjoram are wired in bunches (pages 24-25). Use longer lengths of Eucalyptus, *either wired singly or in pairs.*

▲ *A bouquet of sumptuous summer pickings which can be hung on a wall or door for all to admire.*

You will need:
2 bunches marjoram
2 bunches Ageratum
1 bunch green golden rod
1 bunch Achillea
20 roses

7 peonies
3 heads hydrangea
1 m (1⅛ yd) x 30 cm (12 in) wide silk
Wire 2 peonies singly and 5 small bunches of flowers (pages 24-25). Cover with stem binding tape (page 25).

1 *Gather up a few stems at a time in one hand and wire together just below hand. Continue adding stems, reducing length of extending stems. Secure with wire.*

2 *Make a bow from silk (pages 20-21) and wire to front of bunch.*

3 *Add wired stems and bunches above bow to give fullness, bending forward slightly.*

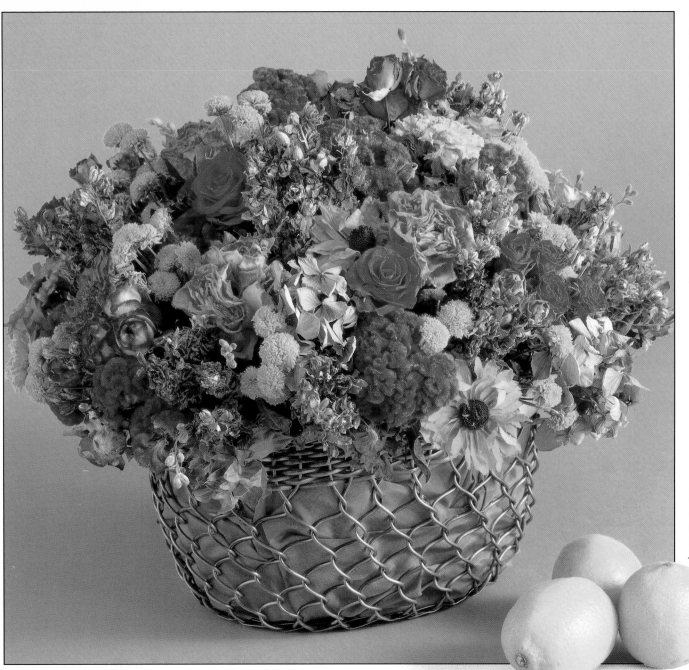

◄ *A Caribbean cocktail of flowers dramatically set off by the deep blue fabric. Line the basket with the latter, laying it flat on the bottom, but draping around the sides. Then add foam and cover with moss. Create your basic shape with wired bunches of blue larkspur (pages 24-25).*

You will need:
3 bunches blue larkspur
2 bunches yellow button chrysanthemums
1 bunch Celosia
1 bunch Carthamus
40 stems red roses ('Jaguar')
7 pink peonies
7 zinnias
2 heads hydrangea

▶ *These dazzling topiaries will bring summer cheer to the home at any time of year. Hair spray will prevent these rather delicate flowers from dropping.*

You will need:
2 birch poles 7.5 cm (3 in) in diameter, 20 cm (8 in) in length
12 bunches cluster-flowered Helichrysum
A little bung moss

1 *Make 2 topiary bases (page 26). Attach a half foam block to each pole. Take one stem of Santolina at a time and trim off heads leaving 2.5 cm (1 in) of stem.*

2 *Wire heads into bunches of 3-4 (pages 24-25).*

3 *Insert bunches into foam as close together as possible. Cover plaster with moss, then spray flowers with hair spray.*

Autumn

The warm tones and mellow shades of autumn are fully exploited in the following designs. Table centrepieces, decorations for walls and doors as well as topiaries feature fiery red chilli peppers, plump and glossy artificial fruits, rich ruby-red glycerined magnolia leaves and the subtle mauve, blue and green hues of the hydrangea.

You will need:
7 bunches red marigolds
2 bunches red peppercorns
1 bunch cones
1 bunch Ageratum
1 bunch roses ('Minuet')
20 chillies

▼ *This arrangement is truly red hot! Wire the peppercorns, Ageratum, roses and marigolds in bunches (pages 24-25). Wire cones and chillies singly. The latter usually have short stems on which to attach the wire (page 35). Make sure that the chillies extend beyond the other elements to create an interesting, spikey outline.*

▶ *Aim for a long, low shape in this arrangement. It would make an excellent centrepiece for a refectory or trestle table - perhaps for a harvest-time or Thanksgiving feast.*

You will need:
5 bunches artificial grapes
1 bunch Ambrosinia
36 assorted roses
35-40 poppy seedheads
9 stems artificial berries
5 stems white paper flowers

Wire flowers with 22 gauge stem wires; artificial grapes with 18 gauge wires (pages 24-25). Cover with stem binding tape (page 25). Leave artificial berries and white paper flowers on original stems.

1 *Cut a block of foam in half to create a shallow full-width piece. Place on a black plastic tray and cover lightly with moss. Tape moss and foam to tray.*

2 *Insert flowers into sides of foam at either end of base. Add berries – 2 at each end, one shorter than the other, 2 along each side and 3 on top of the foam. Fill in with remaining material.*

Autumn

You will need:
1 wooden-framed mirror
40-50 red-dyed magnolia leaves
36 sunflowers
3 m (3⅓ yd) fabric

1 *Drape fabric around mirror frame and glue in place once a good shape has been achieved.*

2 *Cut bases of some of magnolia leaves, apply glue and insert into fabric folds. Group other magnolia leaves and glue onto fabric at intervals. Cut sunflowers from stems as close as possible to the heads. Place at intervals around the frame, some in groups, and glue in place when satisfied with arrangement. Add a few sunflower leaves to lighten the effect.*

◀ *You can transform any plain wooden-framed mirror in this way. Adapt the colour scheme to coordinate with your interior decor by using alternative flowers and fabric.*

▶ *A spectacular topiary destined to be the focal point of any interior. Choose a luxurious fabric in a rich colour for the base.*

You will need:
A branch 7.5 cm (3 in) in diameter, 45 cm (18 in) in length
Thin branches of contorted willow
A large quantity of glycerined magnolia leaves
Bung moss
1 m (1⅛ yd) fabric
Make a topiary base setting the trunk and twigs in plaster (page 26). Attach foam ball to top, cover in wire netting and wire to trunk.

1 *Magnolia leaves come in serveral different sizes. Choose medium-sized leaves. Cut larger leaves to size by trimming the side of the leaf leaving enough stem to wire.*

2 *Hold leaves in groups of 3, splayed slightly at the top. Wire together using 22 gauge wires (pages 24-25). Push into foam ball starting at the top. The right sides of leaves should face inwards. Keep turning topiary while adding bunches of leaves. When complete, wrap pot in fabric tucking raw edges into pot. Cover inside of pot with moss.*

Autumn

1 *Push foam blocks into urn to fill. The middle block should be approximately 5 cm (2 in) higher than others. Cut off top corners using a craft knife.*

2 *Cover foam lightly with moss and pin in place (page 19).*

3 *Place first hydrangea in centre, then a few each side. Fill inbetween with rest of canes. Add wired heads around edge and bend over urn rim.*

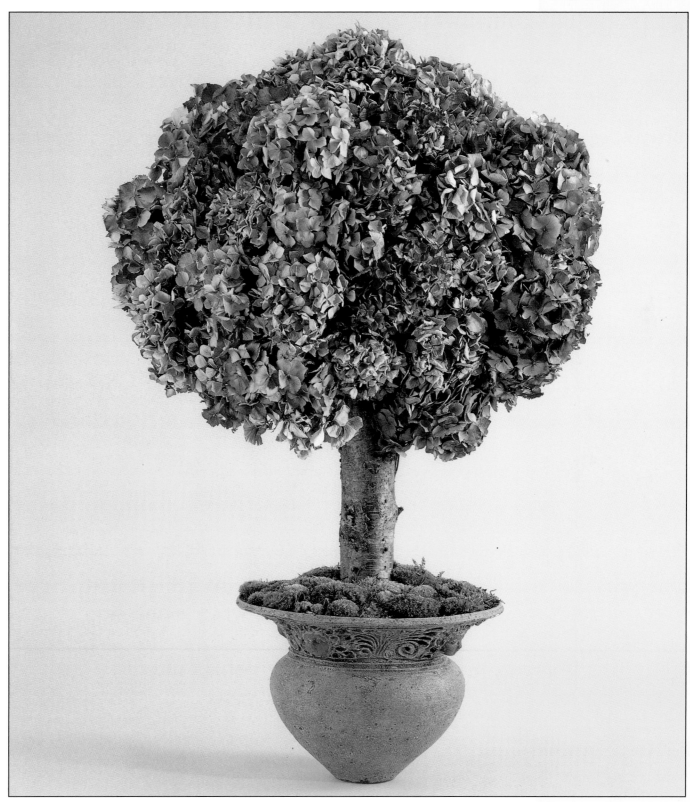

◀ *This arrangement is most effective when different varieties and colours of hydrangea are used in combination.*

You will need:
40 assorted hydrangea heads – 60-70 heads for an all-round arrangement
Wire all except 3-4 hydrangea heads onto green canes; wire remainder with 18 gauge wires (pages 24-25). Bind with brown stem binding tape (page 25).

▶ *You will need approximately 50 hydrangea heads to make this large-scale topiary. Follow the instructions on page 26 to make the topiary base. Insert the trimmed stems of the hydrangea heads into the foam to cover. Cover the plaster in the container with bung moss.*

1 *Bind an 18 gauge wire with stem binding tape and attach to ring for hanging (page 23). Wire woodland drieds into bunches of 3 and bind with tape (page 25). Cut Eucalyptus into 10-12.5 cm (4-5 in) long pieces. Cut proteas from stems leaving 7.5 cm (3 in) of stem. Tie end of a length of green garden twine to ring for binding on stems.*

2 *Place a few stems of Eucalyptus onto ring and bind tightly with twine keeping it taught at all times. Add a couple of proteas, bind tightly then add a woodland bunch. Bind tightly once more. Continue until ring is covered. Make 9 small double-looped bows and 1 large bow for the top (pages 20-21). Insert bows into wreath at intervals.*

◀ *Wire-edged ribbon is excellent for dried flower arranging in that it can be creatively shaped and will remain so.*

You will need:
A straw ring 35 cm (14 in) in
  diameter
5 bunches assorted dried
  woodland items, eg cones, tree
  mushrooms etc
2 bunches dried Eucalyptus
12 proteas
4-5 m (4½-5½ yd) wire-edged
  ribbon

▶ *This magnificient wall plaque makes an original interior decoration. It could be hung horizontally in a suitable location for extra drama.*

You will need:
2 bunches dried grasses
2 bunches morrison
2 bunches glycerined Eucalyptus
1 bunch red species roses
26-30 glycerined magnolia leaves
9 proteas
4 sunflowers
1 string chillies
Wire magnolia leaves in groups of 3 and Eucalyptus *in groups of 5-6 with 22 gauge wires (pages 24-25). Wire grasses and morrison into small bunches. Cover all wires with stem binding tape (page 25). Proteas and sunflowers can remain on original stems.*

1 *To make plaque base, cut foam blocks in half to form 2 shallow pieces. Cut a strip of wire netting slightly longer than 3-4 foam blocks end to end and wide enough to wrap around width of one block.*

2 *Lay wire netting flat and cover lightly with moss. Place blocks onto moss end to end. Bring sides of netting into meet middle top of foam. Twist cut ends of wire together. Make sure netting is tight around foam; if not, tighten at this stage. Cover underside of plaque with plastic (page 20). Attach an 18 gauge wire covered in stem binding tape to the top for hanging (page 23).*

You will need:
9 asssorted roses
6 zinnias
3 m (3⅓ yd) ribbon
Fabric to line basket

▲ Use a piece of silk or satin to line a wire basket. Trim the excess fabric around the rim and using a glue gun, glue the fabric to the rim. Glue the ribbon around the rim to cover, making loops in the ribbon as you work. If the basket is oval, make sure that the ribbon ends meet at one flatter side of the basket. Glue on flowerheads in a group, and a matching group on the opposite side of the basket. Additionally, you could make roses from scraps of the lining fabric by folding and gluing to hold. Intersperse these amongst the dried flowerheads.

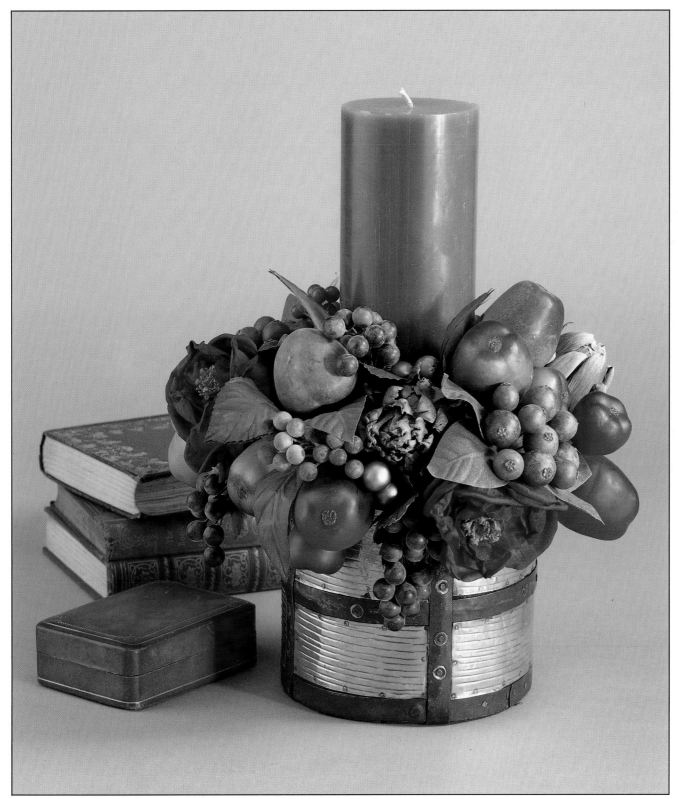

You will need:
6 stems small assorted artificial
  fruits
5 artichokes
3 stems large assorted artificial
  fruits
3 open poly-dried roses
1 candle
If the artificial fruit stem is hand
wrapped, it is best to unravel the
wrapping. In this case you will
have long enough wires on the
undivided fruits not to have to
wire them up.

1 *Cut foam block in half and push*
into pot. Trim corners if too big.
Cover lightly in moss and pin in
place (page 19). Cut a green cane
into 3 pieces and tape to bottom of
candle (page 23). Place centrally.

2 *Cut artificial fruits off stems*
retaining wire stem. Wire large
singly; small in groups of 3 or 5
(pages 24-25). Place artichokes,
fruits then roses.

Winter

Enhance your home in winter with arrangements that are rich and varied in texture whilst subtle in colour combinations. Here we have pots of fragrant herbs to grace the kitchen, a lychin-covered photograph frame that would make a memorable gift and a taste of winter woodland in a natural display of leaves, cones and grasses.

1 *Wrap footed bowl in velvet, wire around neck of bowl (page 19) and cover with ribbon.*

2 *Turn pot upright and tuck excess fabric into top of pot.*

3 *Push foam into bowl to fit tightly, cover with moss and pin in place (page 19). Wire cones and fruit of one stem (pages 24-25 and 97). Other material can remain on original stems.*

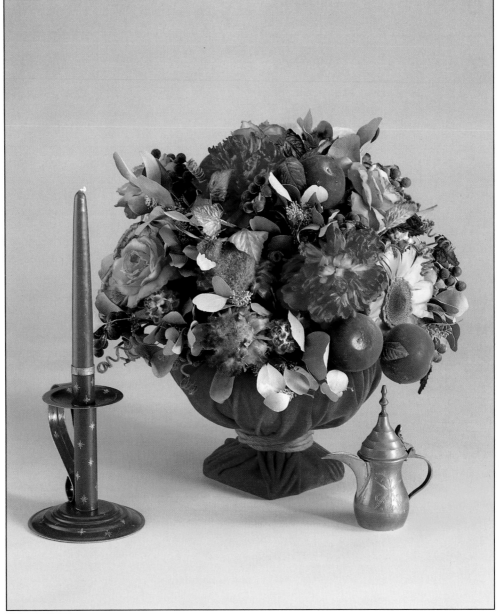

You will need:
2 bunches open cones
1 bunch dry Eucalyptus
1 bunch small cones
3 stems artificial poly-dried peonies
3 stems artificial poly-dried roses
3 stems artificial fruits
3 stems artificial grapes
½ m (½ yd) red velvet
½ m (½ yd) red paper ribbon

▲ *Aim for a fairly solid, high-domed shape when positioning the flowers. Then intersperse the fruits and cones, and lastly the Eucalyptus to lighten the arrangement.*

▶ *The colour and texture of the container is important here, and its roughly-hewn solidity balances the confusion of woodland drieds.*

You will need:
4 bunches assorted woodland cones
2 bunches grasses
1 bunch glycerined beech
5 stems artificial fruits

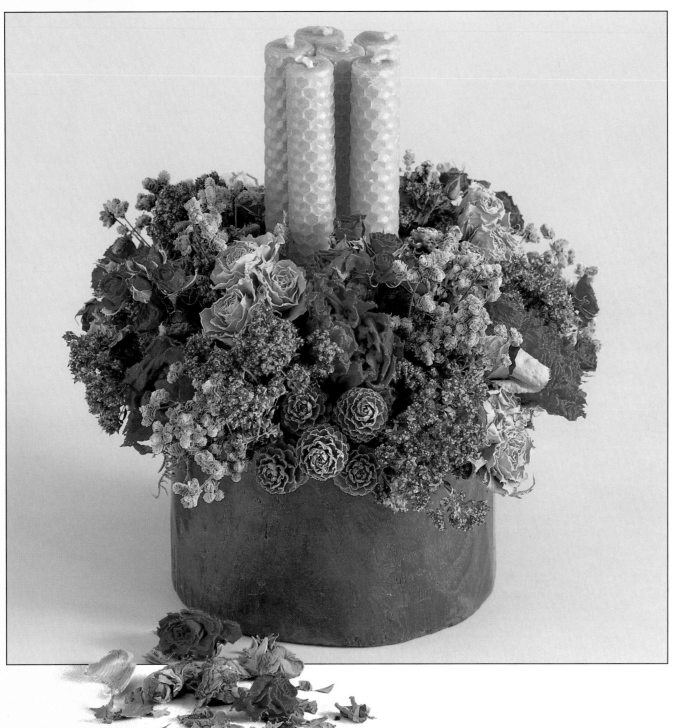

◀ *Bring a warm glow to your winter table with this small beeswax candle arrangement. Fill the container with foam, cover with moss and pin or tape in place (page 19). Insert pieces of green cane into the bottom of the candles (page 23) and group in the centre of the foam. Wire dried items in bunches (pages 24-25), and group to make a 'collar' around the candles, bending the lower bunches well down over the container's edge.*

You will need:
2 bunches woodland cones
1 bunch green marjoram
1 bunch marjoram
20 stems red species roses ('Nikita')
20 stems yellow roses ('Golden Times')
6 narrow beeswax candles

▶ *A charming, compact arrangement suitable for a bedside table. The lavender heads should break out slightly from the otherwise smooth outline.*

You will need:
2 bunches Queen Anne's lace or
*   cow parsley*
1 bunch lavender
1 bunch purple clover
30 assorted roses
2 heads artificial hydrangea
1 stem blue Delphinium

1 *Place small piece of foam into container, cover with moss and tape in place. Wire small bunches of Queen Anne's lace, lavender, roses, clover and Delphinium with 22 gauge wires (pages 24-25). Cut each hydrangea head into 5 pieces. Wire each with 22 gauge wire (pages 24-25). Bind all stems with stem binding tape (page 25). Position about 6 lavender bunches to create basic shape.*

2 *Fill in with remainder of flowers pushing them deeper into foam, if necessary, to make shorter than lavender.*

◀ A commonplace frame for a special family photograph can be immeasurably enhanced by gluing on dried tree lychins. They perfectly echo the yellowing tonal qualities of an ageing black and white photograph.

▶ A winter extravaganza! Pack the bunches of drieds close together to achieve a solid arrangement with a smooth outline.

You will need:
5 bunches Helichrysum
4 bunches Anaphalis (pearl everlasting)
4 bunches red zinnias
3 bunches blue thistles
3 bunches Celosia
3 bunches peach roses
2 bunches red roses
12 heads hydrangea
8 stems artificial fruits
Fill container with foam so that it fits tightly. Shave off corners with a craft knife. Cover lightly with moss.

1 *Wire about 80% of ingredients in groups onto green canes (pages 24-25). Cut fruit from stems (page 97) and wire onto green canes in groups of 3. Wire the remaining material in groups with 18 gauge stem wires (pages 24-25). Cover all wires with stem binding tape (page 25).*

2 *Using 5 items on green canes, create basic shape, ie first bunch in centre top, the other 4 between centre and sides. Position the wired bunches around edge of container. Bend forwards slightly to soften hard edge of pot. Fill in framework with remainder of material on canes.*

1 *Fill vase up to its neck with hydrangea florets.*

2 *Cut approximately three-quarters of a foam block in half lengthways. Cut off bottom corners.*

3 *Foam should fit tightly into vase neck leaving 7.5 cm (3 in) above rim. Fill to rim with florets pushing down sides of foam with round-ended knife.*

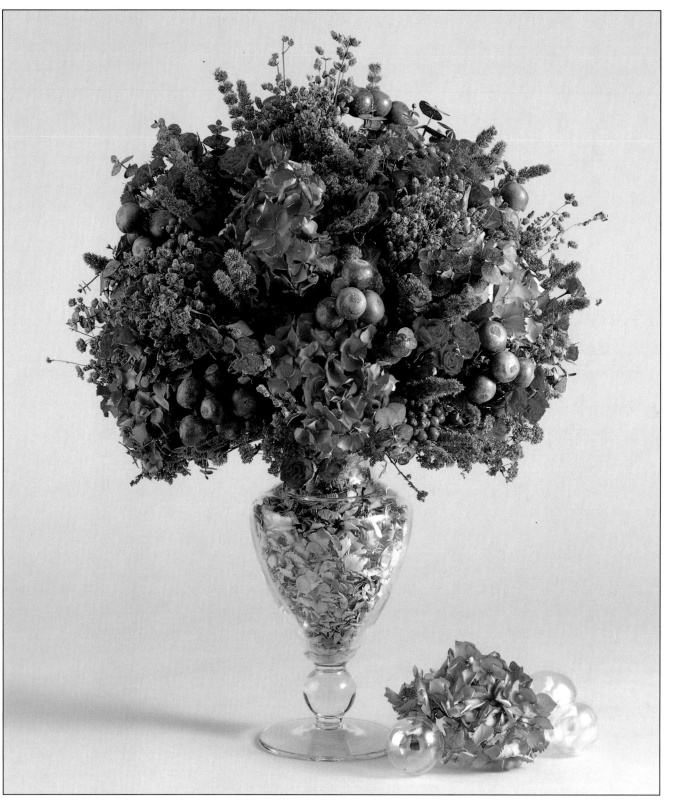

◀ *This arrangement should not be attempted until you are quite confident since the piece of foam is very slender and will begin to disintegrate if stems are repeatedly inserted and removed.*

You will need:
2 bunches green marjoram
2 bunches glycerined Eucalyptus
2 bunches Agastache mexicana
2 bunches dahlias
40 stems dark pink roses
8 stems artificial fruits
4 heads hydrangea
Hydrangea florets
Wire flowers in bunches with 18 gauge wires (pages 24-25); wire hydrangea heads singly. Cut fruits off original stems and wire with 18 gauge wires in groups of 3 (page 97). Cover all wires with stem binding tape (page 25).

▶ *To make this spectacular lavender urn, place a block of foam into the container making sure that at least half of the block is above the pot rim. Round off corners. Divide each lavender bunch into 4 and trim stems to 10-12.5 cm (4-5 in) in length. Wire with 22 gauge wires and bind with stem binding tape (pages 24-25). Place the first bunches at the top of the foam and work downwards keeping the bunches tightly packed.*

1

2

3

▶ *These rustic pots of herbs would make an attractive display in a country kitchen. Group them together and raise one or two pots on split logs, terracotta tiles or bricks to give varying heights. Instructions for making the bay balls are given on page 23.*

You will need:
5 bunches dried marjoram
1 large bunch fresh rosemary
1 large bunch fresh bay
Wire marjoram and rosemary in bunches onto stem wires and cover with stem binding tape (pages 24-25). Bay can be left on original stems.

1 *Cut foam block to fill pots a half to three-quarters full. It should fit tightly.*

2 *Insert bunches one at a time into foam until packed – each herb in a separate pot.*

3 *The low level of foam helps to create the upright nature of the arrangements. Place bay and rosemary pots in a warm, dry place for a week or so.*

Christmas

Dried flowers and seedheads, cones and nuts, cinnamon sticks and artificial fruits can be arranged together to produce a rich array of decorations for the Christmas and New Year celebrations. The following pages feature unique gift wrapping, advent rings of traditional red and gold or cool green and silver, seasonal topiaries that provide a stylish alternative to the usual tree, a magnificent candelabra adorned with fruit and roses, and finally a grand garland for a festive fireplace.

1 *Cut block of foam in half to make a shallow, full-width piece. Place on black tray and cover lightly with moss.*

2 *Tape foam and moss in place. Cut 2 green canes into 6 pieces. Insert 3 pieces into the bottom of each candle (page 23).*

3 *Wire cones with 22 gauge wires (page 25). Mount walnuts onto wires (page 25) and wire together in groups of 5.*

◀ *A traditional centrepiece for the festive table. Beeswax candles give off a sweet, honey-like scent when lit.*

You will need:
11 bunches walnuts
25 assorted cones, one half
   sprayed gold
2 beeswax candles

▲ *Make your Christmas gift packages highly individual and stylish by gluing on nuts, decorative miniature baubles, dried or paper flowers and pumpkin seeds. Glycerined roses (page 16) look sumptuous against a luxury fabric giftwrap. Trail lines of glue over the fabric and sprinkle with glitter. Shake off excess.*

◀ As an unusual alternative to the traditional Christmas tree, why not make an elegant moss topiary which can be decorated with miniature baubles. Follow the instructions on page 26 to make the topiary base, but use a foam cone in place of the ball. Refer to the instructions on page 81 for applying the moss. Glue baubles onto moss to complete. You could make two matching trees to stand either side of a fireplace.

▶ A chunky topiary of plump, glossy artificial fruits which would make a colourful and original table centrepiece for a festive feast.

You will need:
A branch approximately 7.5 cm (3 in) in diameter, 20cm (8 in) in length
100 small artificial fruits
36 large artificial fruits

1 *Set the branch in a bowl using nylon-reinforced plaster (page 26). Cover top of plaster with moss.*

2 *Trim the ends of obling pieces of foam at an angle and glue together to form a large oblong oval shape (page 26). Mount onto branch. Cut fruits from original stems leaving as much stem as possible. Wire large fruits singly with 18 gauge wires; smaller fruits in small and large bunches (pages 24-25). Cover all wires with stem binding tape (pages 25). Position fruits close together in foam. Intersperse artificial leaves.*

1 *Attach fabric to basket rim at 15 cm (6 in) intervals with 22 gauge wires.*

2 *Mount cones onto 18 gauge wires (page 25). Spray with gold paint. Wire bunches of cinnamon together (page 25).*

3 *Attach cinnamon bundles and cones to basket rim with wire 'stems'. Trim excess wires. Tie ribbon around each cinnamon bundle to cover wire.*

▼ *If you wish to fill the basket with pot pourri, line the basket with fabric before you begin.*

You will need:
5 bunches large cinnamon sticks
Approximately 20 cones
1 m (1⅛ yd) fabric
1 m (1⅛ yd) ribbon

▶ *You will need:*
A 30 cm (12 in) diameter foam ring
4 bunches gold grapes
4 bunches lavender
3 bunches marjoram
2 bunches woodland cones touched with gold paint
20-25 stems small red roses

2 stems artificial plums
4 candles and candleholders
2 m (2¼ yd) ribbon
Wire lavender and marjoram in very small bunches with 22 gauge wires (pages 24-25); wire cones. Cover all wires with stem binding tape (page 25).

1 *Position candleholders at equal distances around ring, pushing bases into foam.*

2 *Cut ribbon into 8 equal lengths and make single loop bows without tails (pages 20-21). Place 2 bows by each candleholder.*

3 *Mount candles, then position cones. Add lavender, then marjoram and roses. Complete with plums and gold grapes.*

You will need:
A twig wreath 35 cm (14 in) in
     diameter
Assorted dried cones
Assorted artificial and dried fruits
Walnuts
3 dried corn cobs
1 m (1⅛ yd) ribbon
Cover an 18 gauge wire with stem
binding tape and twist onto
wreath for hanging (page 23).

1 Apply a line of glue from a glue
gun down the length of corn cobs.
Attach at intervals to the wreath.

2 Trim any stem from
pomegranates and other fruits as
close to fruit as possible. Glue the
larger items to wreath. Fill in with
small items until wreath is full
and chunky. Remember to leave
space at top for bow. Make a large
double-looped bow and tie onto
wreath (pages 20-21).

◀ *An unusual yuletide door wreath. It is best to check the position of your items before gluing since they cannot be easily moved once glued.*

▶ *A truly elegant Advent ring. Position candleholders and mount candles. Spray the cones with silver paint and wire (page 25). Wire* Eucalyptus *in bunches and group around the candles. Add cones and fruits. Finally, add the paper flowers to give highlights.*

You will need:
A foam ring 30 cm (12 in) in diameter
3 bunches glycerined Eucalyptus
3 stems white paper flowers
3 stems artificial green plums
18 cones
4 candleholders and candles

1 *Place blocks of foam into dish leaving approximately a 2.5 cm (1 in) margin in which to fit the nuts and moss.*

2 *Place nuts and moss around foam both to hold foam in place and to look attractive.*

3 *Tape cane pieces to bottom of candles (page 23) and place 1 cm (½ in) apart. In order, add hawthorn, fruits, cinnamon. Pin chilli string to foam (page 19).*

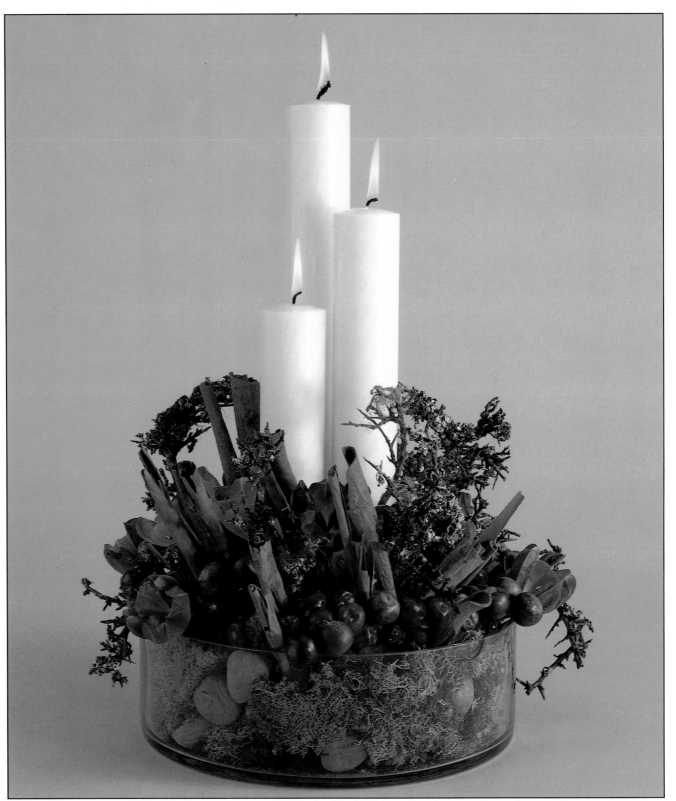

◀ *A highly original candle arrangement which would make a spectacular decoration for a New Year celebration.*

You will need:
1 bunch cinnamon sticks
10 walnuts
8 lychin-covered hawthorn twigs
5 open pods
4 stems artificial fruits
String of round chillies
Lychin moss
3 assorted church candles
Wire hawthorn with 18 gauge wires. Cut fruits from original stems and wire in small bunches (pages 24-25). Cinnamon sticks should be wired singly with 22 gauge wires.

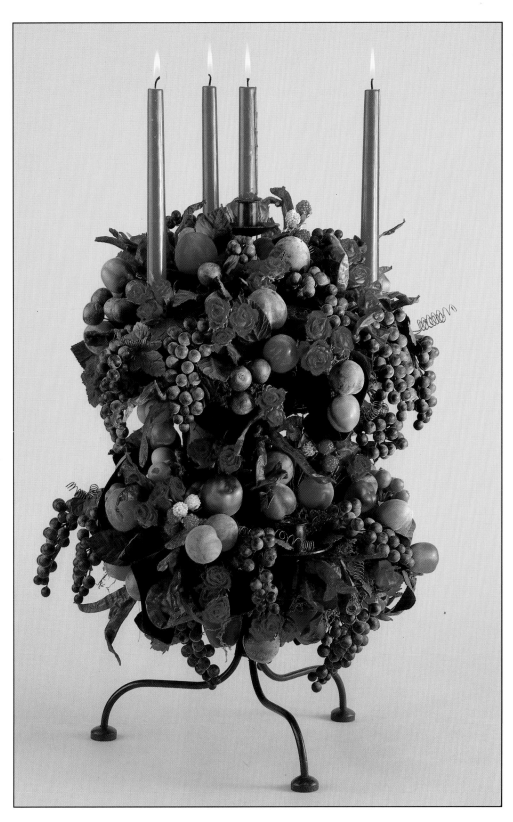

▶ *An extravagant candelabra display for a grand festive gathering. The rich colours of the fruit combine dramatically with the deep red roses. Remember not to leave the arrangement unattended when the candles are lit.*

You will need:
21 bunches artificial grapes
15 bunches chillies
40 red roses
10 stems assorted artificial fruits
4 candles

1 *Place foam blocks on top and bottom levels of candelabra and cover lightly with moss. Cut a circular piece of wire netting and place over foam on top level. Cut a second circle of wire netting, make a cut halfway to the centre and fit around centre stem of candelabra to cover foam. Wire netting securely to edges of 'shelves'.*

2 *Wire roses into groups of 3, chillies in groups of 3-9 and bunches of grapes singly (pages 24-25 and 35). Trim fruits from original stems (page 97) and wire in groups. Position the grapes first, then fruits, roses and finally chillies.*

You will need:
4 terracotta pots
11 bunches gold grapes
5 bunches cinnamon sticks
130-150 walnuts
100 stems red roses
24 cones, 12 sprayed gold
15 woodland cones
12 artificial plums
Lychin and sphagnum moss
5 m (5½ yd) velvet

▶ *Complete this dramatic fireplace display by tying ribbon around the cinnamon bundles so that it covers the wire, and add a large double-looped bow to the centre point of the swag (pages 20-21).*

1 *Make a moss rope (page 20) to form a swag along front of mantelpiece and 'tails' either side. Secure in place with nails or by threading wire through back of mantelpiece. Twist fabric loosely around tube beginning in centre and working outwards. Wire in place at ends of tube. Fill pots with foam and wire with 18 gauge stem wires (page 23). Push wires through moss rope to netting on far side and twist onto wire.*

2 *Mount nuts onto wire stems (page 25) and wire together in large bunches. Fill pots with walnuts and roses. Wire fruits in groups of 3-4, bunches of grapes singly, cinnamon sticks in bunches (pages 24-25) and cones. Wire onto rope, interspersed with clumps of lychin moss.*

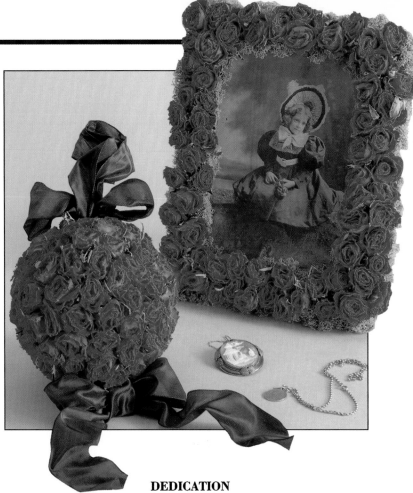

DEDICATION
To my wonderful children, Olivia and Clarence,
who make everything worthwhile.

AUTHOR'S ACKNOWLEDGEMENTS
Topher Faulkner, Hannah Catling, Cherry Clark, Caroline Little,
Angela Chamberlain, Vanessa Lee, Sarah Eastwood, Donna Henderson, Francis Bearman
and Jo Finnis without whom none of this would have been possible.
Dried flowers: *Robson Whatley, R & R Flowers, Machin & Henry, Tudor Rose*;
silk flowers: *Best Blooms, H Andreas, Austin & Co, Forever Flowers*;
sundries: *Cocquerels* and *Peter Harvey*.

All products used in this book are available from Veevers Carter Flowers,
125 Sydney Street, London SW3, tel: 071 370 0549.

CREDITS
Editorial: Jo Finnis
Design: Alison Jewell
Photography: Steve Tanner
Photographic Direction: Nigel Duffield; Jo Finnis
Illustration: Geoff Denney Associates
Typesetting: Julie Smith
Production: Ruth Arthur; Sally Connolly; Neil Randles
Director of Production: Gerald Hughes